C000083226

# DUCATI
*PEOPLE*

# DUCATI
## PEOPLE

*EXPLORING THE PASSION BEHIND THIS LEGENDARY MARQUE*

Kevin Ash  *Foreword by* **Michaela Fogarty**

# DucatiPeople

### Azzolini
Agata

14

### Bisceglia
Leonarda

20

### Bordi
Massimo

26

### Castiglioni
Claudio

32

### Cazzato
Anna Maria

38

### Clarke
Chris

42

### Farnè
Franco

46

### Fogarty
Carl

50

### Forni
Andrea

58

### Francolini
Luca

64

### Gross
David

68

### Lodi
Livio

74

Mengoli
Gianluigi

80

Minoli
Federico

88

Montemaggi
Marco

94

Neilson
Cook

98

Perry
Suzi

104

Schelter
Kristin

110

Smart
Paul

116

Taglioni
Fabio

124

Tamburini
Massimo

134

Tardozzi
Davide

140

Terblanche
Pierre

146

Wynne
Steve

154

# Michaela Fogarty

**Foreword**

This is more like a family album than a book, as far as I'm concerned. I've spent most of the last ten years living with Ducati and during that time the company has changed a lot, especially since the takeover by TPG in 1996. But one aspect hasn't changed at all. When I first became involved with Ducati I was impressed at how family-oriented it all was, and the change of ownership didn't make the slightest difference to that. Ducati has always been an intimate, personal company that has made me feel very much a part of the family. This is quite different from other race teams I've been around when Carl was racing for them.

Ducati helped make my life so much easier when Carl was racing. My only way of coping with the thought that in his job, any weekend he might not ever come home again, was to be right there on the pit wall, cheering him on and watching him come round on every lap, going through it all with him. And Ducati was always there to make sure I was OK.

They could be frustrating at times – they have to talk, talk, talk before actually doing anything! We'd spend hours discussing which restaurant to go to instead of just getting in the car and going there! But maybe that is all part of being Italian. And to be a true family you must have character, and this was a part of it.

My feelings about Ducati really came out when Carl retired after his crash in Australia in 2000. I had been thinking I would be the happiest person on earth when he finished – all the travelling was getting me down and I was always worried about his safety. But I was more upset than he was! I'd been living with this wonderful family for so long, and suddenly it was all cut off. They had to go on of course, to the next championship round, and we had to be left behind, although Davide Tardozzi offered to stay with us. It was like a bereavement, but they still make us feel so welcome when we come back.

I truly want to thank Ducati, first for believing in Carl, then for letting Carl and me be a part of the family. We will never forget the days we had with them. If anyone can capture the essence of what it is that makes Ducati so special it is Kevin Ash. Carl and I know him as an excellent journalist with the honesty needed to report the lows as well as the highs, which is the only way of presenting the full picture of this unique and special company.

Ducati embraced two Fogartys when it signed Carl. Michaela always felt a member of the Ducati family. (Gold & Goose)

For a motorcycle journalist it's important to maintain a level of impartiality when dealing with the wide, fascinating and still-growing spectrum of companies involved in this business. But like many other observers, I have always found it difficult not to get caught up in the special atmosphere surrounding one factory in particular. Ducati certainly has some elements easily invoked as reasons for the passions it arouses: its home is in Italy, the country where the world of cars and motorcycles vies with religion itself as the national template for how people should live their lives. Ducati too has a rich and fabulously successful racing heritage on which it continues to build rather than relying solely on past glories and nostalgia – instead this is woven into the current machines, lending them an authenticity which others have either forgotten or have yet to accrue. And the bikes themselves are a pure, rich red, the colour long associated with Italian motorsport success and history, as well as being the hue of blood, passion, speed and aggression.

But there's more to Ducati even than these attributes. It's a company which adheres to particular values in the design of its machines, in the completeness of the motorcycle rather than the pursuit of power alone and, successful or not, it deserves respect for this. Ducati has its own unique engineering solutions, a valuable asset in a sphere where enthusiasts' technical awareness is far greater than in most other fields: the famous desmodromic valve operating system is complemented by faith in the 90 degree V-twin engine and the steel trellis frame.

Ducati has attracted some of the greatest engineers and designers in motorcycling history, including Fabio Taglioni, Massimo Bordi and Massimo Tamburini. Now add to these the clinching factor: Ducati's status as the underdog, the small, usually cash-strapped enthusiast factory battling against the might and money, first of the established European concerns, then of the high-technology, big-resource Japanese companies who swept all before them.

Almost all. Ducati V-twins have dominated World Superbike racing against all-comers for more than a decade, the series to which motorcyclists can most closely relate their own road-going machines. Ducati has repeatedly displayed a rare ability to make people gasp, to astonish and to shake motorcycling to its core. The race victories of Paul Smart at Imola in 1972, Cook Neilson in 1977, Mike Hailwood in 1978 and any number of wins and championships by Carl Fogarty have

The most famous race of all time – Mike Hailwood takes his Ducati 900SS to victory at the Isle of Man, 1978. (B.R. Nicholls)

left onlookers breathtaken, while the unveiling of the stunningly beautiful 916 and utterly original Monster M900 had observers speechless. This book is not a history of Ducati. There are plenty of those which, like Ian Falloon's *The Ducati Story* and *Ducati Super Sport* (Haynes), do the job admirably. They tell how the company was started in 1926 when the three Ducati brothers – Bruno, Adriano and Marcello – founded the Societé Scientifica Radio Brevetti Ducati to produce electrical equipment, including radios, using designs patented by their father Antonio Ducati. After the Second World War, bound by restrictions on what they were allowed to produce, the trio decided to address the urgent market for cheap transport and in 1946 produced the Cucciolo, a simple four-stroke engine which strapped onto a bicycle. Soon they were building complete motorcycles and, being Italian, inevitably started to race.

After rapid growth, followed some time later by years of decay under Italian state ownership, Ducati was teetering near to extinction: 'a tiny little flame was all that was left' recalls technical director Gianluigi Mengoli. Then, with production down to less than 3,000 bikes a year, you could almost hear the blast of bugles as the cavalry charged to the rescue in the form of another family concern, the Castiglioni brothers, Claudio and Gianfranco, who had initially bought engines from Ducati for their Cagiva bikes. Later still of course, despite the Castiglionis' passionate commitment, the marque was floundering again. This time help came from American venture capitalists. The fear now was that Ducati would be asset-stripped and dumped – workers, customers, fans and much of Italy it seemed viewed the takeover with hostility. In fact the marque has been reborn.

This book looks at men and women whose lives have been touched by or, as is so often the case, completely dominated by Ducati. Some are the well-known figures who have helped to shape the marque. Others work for the company, have their own sphere of influence or have in turn been influenced by Ducati.

Each chapter is dedicated to just one of these people. We hear from Leonarda Bisceglia, a test rider with a dream job, Massimo Bordi, the engineering genius who seemed to sense what customers wanted, Anna Maria Cazzato, the administrative director who talks of the soul of the company, and Chris Clarke who, after 22 years as an often exasperated dealer, feels that under its

new ownership Ducati 'is in serious danger of getting it right'. This warmth seems to be pretty universal. People love Ducati. They love their involvement. Discovering the Apollo prototype was 'my personal odyssey' says Livio Lodi, assistant curator at the Ducati Museum, a pivotal place, a visit to which is, for many fans, something of a religious experience.

Tough business folk get almost poetic when dealing with Ducati. Federico Minoli, put in overall charge by the Texas Pacific Group when it bought the Ducati Group of companies in 1996, realised that they had acquired something 'very precious – these are brands or products that mean something extra to a niche of very passionate people'.

David Gross, the New York corporate lawyer closely involved in the deal, says 'it was like finding some great undiscovered jewel!' That jewel exerts a far-reaching appeal. 'I wasn't born here, Italian isn't my main language, my family isn't here, and I've come thousands of miles to work at Ducati,' says South African Pierre Terblanche. As head of design, he bears an awesome responsibility with such seminal machines as the 916 setting the company's standards, a bike that has been named motorcycle of the century in many polls, which has dominated World Superbike racing, and which appears in museums, design exhibitions and fashion magazines, acclaimed for its beauty, poise and performance: 'We have to match up to these things and also to move forward in every respect, especially in ergonomics and aerodynamics.' BBC race commentator Suzi Perry adds her own privileged and perceptive insight into the workings of the Ducati race team and explains why in every picture of her with a motorcycle the bike is always a Ducati. She notes the special energy in the Ducati pit garage – 'it's so alive'. Even today's fire-breathing race

Fabio Taglioni and wife Narina played host to Ducati visitors Livio Lodi, Ludovica Benedetti and Agata Azzolini. (Kevin Ash)

machines can trace their roots back to Fabio Taglioni's last complete design, the Pantah-based 750F1. Hence the telephone call to Taglioni after the 2001 Italian round of the WSB championship. It came from the security guard on the factory gate who was so caught up in the passion of racing that he wanted to congratulate the architect of Ducati's history on this latest victory.

'At Ducati we're like a family and Taglioni was our grandfather,' says Davide Tardozzi, the Ducati WSB team manager who is something of a legend himself, well known for being the man who put the fight back into Fogarty when he seemed to be faltering in 1998. In writing this book I have been privileged to meet a number of Ducati people and hear about their lives, their views and their perspective on the workings of the Bologna factory, past and present, with the aim of painting a more complete picture of what fuels the so-obvious passion Ducati motorcycles generate around the world.

The opinions are sometimes contradictory, occasionally critical – there's no Ducati censorship here so the bad, where it exists, is aired as freely as the good. And that's exactly as it should be, especially as so many of our subjects insist that it is Ducati's faults and mistakes which complement and work with its glories and successes in inspiring such widespread, genuine feeling. The ups are that much higher for the downs and without one or the other, there would be no room for character. Even today, with Ducati financially more secure than at any time in its history, not everyone is in agreement that it has chosen the right path. Massimo Bordi, who has arguably been at least as influential as Taglioni himself and who underlined Ducati's ability to shock with his dramatic departure in 2001, explains in detail the reasons why he had to leave. Against this

The 2001 WSB Champion Troy Bayliss returned to Imola with his bike in Paul Smart replica colours. Sadly he crashed. (Ducati)

Federico Minoli counters with his persuasive arguments in favour of the course Ducati is taking today. Suzi Perry compares Ducati with an Italian soap opera. The difference is, this is for real. It's not just larger than life – for many, many enthusiasts around the world, it *is* life.

Most of the people who have co-operated with the compiling of this book are also featured in it, so my thanks go out to all who gave up their time to be subjected to interviews, photographs, phone calls and e-mails. I shan't detail them here – turn the pages for a complete list. But one person in particular who is not featured deserves my special thanks. Without the unstinting effort and unlimited patience of Ludovica Benedetti, Ducati's press officer responsible for keeping us foreign journalists informed and happy, this book would have taken ten times the effort and time to put together.

Thank you too to Agata Azzolini who endured my company for so long in her professionally executed task as translator, compensating for my embarrassing ignorance of the Italian language and bringing home to me, as tears rolled down her face in our desperately moving interview with Fabio and Narina Taglioni, just how deep is her passion for the Bologna brand. That's why I decided to feature her in the book – how could I leave her out?

I'm grateful to Michaela Fogarty for her heart-felt foreword. With typical generosity she is donating her fee to the fund to help the families of the New York firemen killed on 11 September. A mention too must go to my wife Caroline for her patient acceptance of the laptop computer which accompanied us everywhere, even on holiday, and to Mark Hughes, Flora Myer and Simon Larkin at Haynes Publishing.

But most of all, my gratitude and my heart goes out to Narina Taglioni. Only weeks after I spent a long and privileged afternoon with her and her husband, Fabio Taglioni died. What you will read in the Taglioni chapter was only made possible because of Narina, as Fabio was unable to speak following an operation on his throat. Her knowledge of his past is utterly comprehensive, yet it is her sheer vivacity and humour which will remain with me, as will her so-obvious deep devotion to her husband. Motorcycling has lost its greatest engineer and visionary, but far more important than that, Narina has lost the husband she clearly loved so much.

W ith a name like Agata Azzolini you might assume this young woman would have an inclination towards Italian motorcycles. But that's not how it started, and it doesn't explain the near fanatical zeal with which Agata immerses herself in all things to do with the marque. Nor why she decided one day simply to fly to Italy to turn up at the Ducati factory just to see if she could get a job there. Any job. Agata wasn't even born in Italy, but Shrewsbury in England, although both her parents are Italian. Her Sicilian father was working in the UK as a bricklayer, while her mother had run away from her Italian home to become a nun in England. She went as far as entering a convent before falling ill and leaving, after which she worked in an (Italian) ice-cream company in Shrewsbury, where she met Agata's father, a story in itself worthy of a chapter in a book.

But not this one, because neither of Agata's parents had – or have – the slightest interest in motorcycles of any description, and indeed never even owned a car, so Agata's early years were spent with less exposure to the motor culture than even a typical English child. Agata's Italian heritage was certainly not ignored – until she went to school she spoke almost entirely in Italian – but it was not a life in which Ferraris, Ducatis or even Fiats and Vespas made any sort of impression on the family.

So maybe this Italian fascination for cars and motorcycles and the history associated with them comes with a gene which sometimes skips a generation. It was certainly not environment which turned Agata into the incurable Ducati fanatic she is today, so the only explanation is some natural proclivity. If so, it lay dormant until she was 14, when in what she describes as a pivotal moment in her life, she opened a page of a magazine and saw an advert for a little Honda. 'It was a full page ad', she says. 'There was a CB125 on its stand with a girl standing next to it, no crash helmet or anything. She just looked so incredibly cool, and I thought, I want to be that girl!'

But she does look back on that time with some embarrassment: 'Oh dear yes. I used to really like custom bikes! Horrible things, but I was only young... And I was into heavy rock music too – I could so easily have become a tattooed biker chick, and I'm so glad I didn't go that route now.'

She didn't go any route at all for quite some time, as it turned out her father was worse than

Agata Azzolini, on her 748 at the factory. 'I used to like custom bikes...but I was only young!' (Kevin Ash)

A bike fanatic who
just had to work for Ducati . . .

Agata wasn't allowed a motorcycle until she left home – her parents thought them much too dangerous. (Kevin Ash)

Agata longs for the day
when Ducati decides to
make a road version of
her favourite Duke, the
Supermono. (Kevin Ash)

uninterested in motorcycles, he was actively against them. 'I think he'd ridden a bike at some point and had had some sort of accident on one, and decided they were much too dangerous. So I wasn't allowed to have one or to have much to do with them while I was still at home.' Then when she was 19, she had a boyfriend who owned a Honda CG125 – hardly a superbike, but it was a motorcycle. The results were a little disappointing: 'Of course I had to have a go on it. And guess what, I was absolutely useless! I couldn't turn corners at all – I'd just keep riding in a straight line until I hit a kerb or something, then fall off.

But it didn't put me off at all. I'd just go out on the back instead, although I don't think I was supposed to do that on a bike with learner plates...'

In retrospect, it's quite surprising that Agata is with us at all, as at 21, when she'd left home, she bought a Honda CD200. The law at the time restricted learners to engines up to 125cc, unless the motorcycle had a sidecar attached. So with the 200cc Honda she bought a device called a Sidewinder, a vestigial sidecar with tiny wheel which pivoted so the bike could be leaned in either direction, just like a solo. It was purely a law-dodging device, designed to be bolted on and practically forgotten about.

Which is exactly what Agata did: 'I decided, after several near misses, when I completely forgot the Sidewinder and crashed it into my boyfriend's Honda VFR750 as I pulled up alongside that I was too dangerous with it, so got rid of the CD200 and bought a Honda CB125 – just like the bike in that advert which had such a big influence on me all those years ago.

'But I was lethal on that! I just didn't like changing gear, or more specifically, I couldn't get changing down right, so I hardly ever bothered changing up – my boyfriend was always shouting at me for screaming about with the engine revving like mad!' But despite all this, Agata's love for bikes was now deep-rooted. The speed and freedom she found addictive and she bought every motorcycle magazine she could. There's one she remembers clearly now: 'I bought a copy of *Performance Bikes* in 1987, and it had a review of the Ducati 900SS, the red and white one. I just thought wow, that's one heck of a bike, I've got to have one!'

Meanwhile, Agata managed to avoid killing herself on a series of other machines from a Kawasaki GPZ500S to a 'horrible' Yamaha FZ600, followed by Honda's CBR600 and VFR750. 'But all the time now I was thinking about Ducatis. I even went to have a look at an 851 Tricolore, but in the event I was put off it by the 16-inch front wheel, which everyone said made the handling feel odd.'

Then after a brief time with a Honda CBR400 – which was just too slow – Agata bought her first Ducati, a new 900SS. 'I should have been put off for life as the carburettors iced up as soon as I got it,' she says. 'It was winter and wet and the engine kept cutting in and out on one cylinder, which was really dangerous. But the shop fixed that, and I found myself just loving the sound and the feel of the bike. I owned that for a year, then bought a gorgeous yellow Superlight 900SS, after which I ordered a 916!'

It took a year for Agata's 916 to arrive – Ducati was having serious cash-flow problems and production was badly disrupted because suppliers were holding back deliveries until they'd been paid – but Agata didn't get on with it straight away: 'I couldn't get used to the riding position at first – it felt like I was going to be tipped over the front as soon as I touched the brakes, but I took it out on a race track almost as soon as I got it, and everything started to feel right after that.'

Agata's devotion to the marque had another barrier to overcome – she's only just over five feet tall and simply can't reach the ground on a standard 916. So she fitted a shorter Penske rear shock and bought a special seat unit as well as lowering the front end so she could keep her bike upright when stationary.

But she wasn't happy with just riding the bike: 'I became a complete Ducati anorak! I bought

all the books I could, read all the magazines and became more and more fascinated with the history of the company, which I love. It has everything. The 916 is breathtakingly beautiful, and there it was as well winning the World Superbike Championship with Fogarty, while there was this amazing engineer called Taglioni who you could trace the 916 back to.

'Then came another important moment for me. I was out on another track day with my 916 and there were lots of other Ducatis going around. I was riding with them, listening to the sound, admiring the looks, and I decided I wanted to get properly involved with Ducati. So I flew to Bologna!' Agata had already met Marco Montemaggi, the museum curator, at a Ducati Owners' Club dinner, but without any job being promised flew out anyway.

In fact she pitched rather higher than Montemaggi when she arrived: 'When I was outside the gate I decided to phone Massimo Bordi! Amazingly, I got him on the phone and he agreed to see me, but then his meeting ran very late and he couldn't. But I still got a job, working as a guide in the museum!

'People were always amazed when they were faced with this young woman showing them around who knew so much about Ducati!' Eventually Agata had to return to England, but her first task here was to buy herself a yellow 748 (lowered, like her 916 had been), which she now rides everywhere. But she's determined to return to some sort of involvement with Ducati: 'I was in hog's heaven at the museum. It was wonderful, and I will go back to doing something with Ducati, I don't care what.'

For goodness sake Ducati, just employ her again will you?

It took some persuasion to remove Agata from the 996R, and the bike's only in a noise emissions chamber! (Kevin Ash)

In a country where a local mayor only recently was able to ban what were perceived as 'ugly women' from baring too much of themselves during the hot summer months in his town near Rimini for fear of putting off tourists, you can imagine a typical factory shop floor in Italy is hardly at the forefront of the battle against chauvinism.

Indeed, in Ducati's Bologna plant an effective measure of a woman's attractiveness is the volume of the wolverine howls which follow her should she brave a walk along one of the production lines. It's a male dominated working environment feeding a male dominated market, in a country which has been – how shall we put it? – a little slower than some to take political correctness to its heart. Which is why even the most right-on fighter for sexual egalitarianism will struggle not to raise, at the very least, an eyebrow at the motorcycle testing area sited at the end of the Monster and superbike production lines.

In amongst the swarthy, depressingly good-looking examples of Italian masculinity which you'd expect to find in such a place, one of the standard issue Ducati red boiler suits fails dismally to disguise an altogether different shape, its problem compounded by a belt pulling in the surplus material around a narrow waist. It's a profile as unmistakably feminine as the plan view of a 916, and it belongs to Leonarda Bisceglia, a woman so happy in her job the only thing she can imagine swapping it for is a similar job in a different department at Ducati.

Lea, as she prefers to be known, is one of a small team of testers whose job is . . . well, if you have an envious nature, you might want to skip the next line. Lea's job is to ride around Italy on Ducatis. There's rather more to it than just that, but it is fundamental to what she does, as she explains: 'What we're doing is testing all aspects of the bikes which are currently in production. We will select a machine off the production line, then go through our testing procedures.

'I must ride every bike for 10,000km. After that I measure the wear on all sorts of components, especially the consumables such as the brake pads, the clutch plates and so on. I also check the oil level in the engine and inspect the forks and shock absorber closely for signs of wear or leakage past the seals, and a host of other things which might show signs of wear or damage.

'I also run the bike on the dynamometer to check how the engine's power has changed, and

Most people do this for pleasure, but Leonarda Bisceglia's *job* is to take this 998 out for a blast. (Kevin Ash)

Just the **bike**, the road and me
– the test rider with a **dream** job

measure the content of the exhaust gases so changes inside the engine can be noted.'

When Lea's finished she writes up a full report on the bike, which is passed on to another tester who corrects any problems, replaces any consumables near the end of their life and who then adds another 10,000km to the machine.

This way Ducati keeps in touch with how its machines and those components supplied from outside sources (which is the majority of parts) are performing in everyday conditions, as well as in a laboratory test environment. Lea covers the whole of Ducati's range, from 750SS to Monster to 748 and even the limited edition 996R superbike, although she hadn't had a chance to give Troy Bayliss's factory racer a go when we spoke to her: 'Oh yes, I'd love to ride it, but there's not much chance of that, is there?' Mind you, with her looks she could probably give Bayliss himself a bit of a workout if she wanted? 'Hmm, or maybe Ben Bostrom...? Maybe he's a little young for me though.'

Still, it's something to think about when she's out riding, which she prefers to do alone. 'I often get irritated when I'm riding with other people. They're always messing around on the roads, or they want to stop and have a coffee or something. It's perfection for me when there's just the bike, the road and me, and nothing else to interfere.'

Lea can ride more or less wherever she likes, just as long as she put the miles – or kilometres, they're not fussy – on the machines, and says she prefers to head for the twisty mountain roads, as they're so much more interesting than the autostrade or town routes.

But the images are not all idyllic visions of a beautiful Italian woman astride a blood red

Leonarda is settled in and happy in her job now, but it took a while for her to be accepted in a male environment. (Kevin Ash)

Ducati driving her way up a spectacular mountain pass in the blazing sunshine (some of them are though – you just can't help it...). It rains in Italy too, and in winter it gets very cold. And when most Ducati owners are tucking up their steeds cosily until the arrival of spring, Lea is still out there, putting at least her required 500km minimum a week under the wheels of yet another Ducati and occasionally as much as 1,000km in a day.

How does she cope with that? 'I look like the Michelin Man,' she laughs. 'But I don't mind that at all as I don't like all the fuss that comes with being a woman on a motorcycle. I always plait my hair before I go out for a ride and tuck it into my jacket. It's to stop it blowing all over the place in the wind and getting tangled, but it also means people don't recognise me as a woman.

'In the first year I was doing this I rather liked the attention – it's nice to have men notice you, of course. But then it just became a nuisance, and now when I'm riding I don't even stop for a coffee because I get fed up with all the comments when I take my crash helmet off.'

How do the men at work cope with her as a test rider? 'At first when I started this job two years ago they were very hostile, always looking out for any mistakes I might make, and they looked down on me.

'But that's really changed now. They have a lot of respect for me as I've proved I can do the job, and I'm not excluded or anything.'

She didn't have the easiest start though. Still she squeals in horror at one particular memory: 'I had only just started, and I had an ST4 to ride. Normally I get off the bike before putting down the sidestand, but for some reason I tried to get the stand down while still sitting on the bike. And I fell off!' Presumably you couldn't pick it up again? 'Oh, it was worse than that! My leg was trapped under the bike and I couldn't even get myself up! I just had to lay there until someone came to help.'

Where was this?

'It was in the car park!' She screws up her eyes in embarrassment.

A car park? So people saw you do it?

'Not *a* car park! *The* car park. The one at the front of the factory! And everyone was looking

Leonarda reckons she's
not recognised as a
woman when she's on a
motorcycle in her winter
riding gear... (Kevin Ash)

out at me because I was new to the job!' We pause for a few minutes while Lea and the two other women present at the interview bury their faces and make screeching noises – it seems like the only thing to do.

I try to calm Lea's involuntary spasms and help her uncurl her toes by moving on to her previous jobs. It turns out she'd been at Ducati for two years before she fell off the ST4... sorry, started in her current position, working on the production lines doing everything from engine assembly to the chassis lines, fuel tanks and so on.

Before that she worked at an underwear factory...

Down boys! Not, as you might expect, modelling lingerie, but in the packing department. This was in the far south of Italy where, as her dark looks and compellingly warm and vivacious nature suggest, Lea was born and brought up, something she's fiercely proud of. When the factory ran into hard times she had the choice of severance pay or to move north and work at the Ducati factory in Bologna.

As she'd been passionate about motorcycles since she was 15 it wasn't a difficult decision – the first bike she'd ridden had been a KTM, which belonged to her boyfriend's father, a national level motocross rider. 'I loved that, but I fell off it and destroyed my knees!' But Ducati means a lot to Lea, even aside from employing her. 'Ducati is a very special company. I know a lot about the history, and I also know a lot about the suppliers, where the shock absorbers come from and stuff like that. I'd actually like to know more about that side of the history, what the shock absorbers were like in Taglioni's day, how things have progressed, that sort of thing.'

If anyone could be excused for having had enough of motorcycles at the end of a working day, it would be Lea. Far from it. Hers might be, as she describes it, '...a dream job. It's the ultimate. The only thing that could be better anywhere would be working for Forni in the prototype testing department!' So what does she have of her own, in her garage at home? 'A Monster! Of course!'

Of course...

It must be every motorcycle factory's dream to have an engineering visionary and genius working for it at some point in its history, although few are this lucky. Yet Ducati has had two. Better still, the arrival of Massimo Bordi as Fabio Taglioni headed towards the end of his career really could not have been timed any better.

Bordi's fascination with engines started when he was a small boy hanging around his uncle's workshop before tinkering with and then tuning engines himself with his friends. He pored through all the books he could get on cars and motorcycles, and by the age of 17 had acquired both a serious passion for the subject, deciding that he would become an engineer, and his first Ducati. It was this which fed his particular fascination for the desmodromic valve system, so at university in Bologna in 1973, for his final year's thesis he chose to combine this with his interest in Cosworth's four-valve cylinder head ideas and investigate the design of the desmodromic four-valve head. As part of his research he went to Ducati to discuss the idea with Taglioni, who helped him although against the idea in principle. Bordi explains why: 'Taglioni told me he'd done his own tests on four-valve cylinder heads and didn't get good results. But the angle between the inlet and exhaust valves he'd used was very wide and the inlet manifolds were not straight, which was basically a mistake.' Another difficulty was the great complication of fitting the desmodromic system for four valves within the confines of a cylinder head, which Taglioni had decided was too much of a problem. Bordi however was convinced this was the way ahead, but it was to be some time before he could prove his point.

He'd applied successfully to join Ducati in 1976 – 'I thought I stood a better chance of getting a job here than Ferrari, which I'd also considered.' But Bordi only worked there for three months before he was called up for Italian military service. He couldn't have stayed at Ducati anyway because there were many jobs being cut at the time. Then in 1978 he was called back by Taglioni, only to be very disappointed at how the job worked out. 'Taglioni had said to me I'd be working on bikes. But engineer Martini joined the day before me and he was put on to them instead. I think it was because he was from Romagna like Taglioni, and I was from Umbria,' laughs Bordi. 'But the times weren't so good at first. From 1978 to 1980 Ducati was in big trouble, and I was

Massimo Bordi ponders the way forward for Ducati. His ideas clashed with the owners' and now he's left. (Kevin Ash)

The engineering genius who knew what customers wanted

put to work on the diesel engines. I did some bike work though – I increased the capacity of the Pantah from 600cc to 750cc and did the TT2 and F1 versions, as well as increasing the capacity of the older bevel drive engine, and doing the gearbox and clutch on that.'

Ducati's position looked increasingly precarious in the early 1980s as the owners decided to increase diesel engine production at the expense of the motorcycles, but the arrival of the Castiglionis and their Cagiva Group changed all that, first with their large orders for engines in 1983, then when they bought Ducati in 1985. Bordi remembers the time as one of complete change: 'It was thanks to them that Ducati could grow again. A lot of big projects all went ahead – the big version of the Pantah engine, the new water-cooled two valve engine (which went in the Paso), and the new 851.' Gianluigi Mengoli describes how this evolved in the chapter dedicated to him, how he and Bordi had been developing this in secret, in their spare time at home. The relationship between the two was much as it would have been in the open though effectively with Mengoli acting as senior project manager while the idea and fundamental design came from Bordi, the technical director. The two men saw the project past its difficult early stages, when as the 748ie endurance bike, its power output was little different to the racing Pantah engine, and with the new Castiglioni money Bordi was able to take it out to 851cc.

'Taglioni was not pleased with this,' says Bordi. 'He said it would be a disaster. In 1986 he even arranged a press conference to make it quite clear this engine was not his responsibility and he wanted nothing to do with it! He was very quiet about that later...' This was the engine which grew into the 888, the 916 and all its derivatives, and which has dominated World Superbike racing throughout the existence of the series. It's given credibility to the V-twin engine generally and has been so effective, even Honda has copied the layout after failing to beat it convincingly. There's no question, Bordi's engine is one of the great motorcycle engineering achievements of the last century, made all the more incredible by the circumstances in which it was first designed and considering the resources available to the small Ducati company in comparison to its far bigger and wealthier rivals.

Shortly before the Cagiva takeover, Taglioni had retired and Bordi had moved into his position

Bordi's fascination with engines goes back as far as he can remember and beyond: aged three on a Lambretta. (Ducati)

as Ducati's technical director, which amuses him now: 'When this happened Ducati was still a part of the VM Group which made diesel engines, and I was put in charge of the engineering partly because of the experience I had gained with diesels in those first years, when I had been so disappointed. I was in Taglioni's position and I was also Martini's boss!'

After the Castiglionis' arrival, Bordi found himself not just in charge of Ducati's engineering and model development, but with the funding to carry forward all his ideas, and as a consequence, that 851 engine proved to be only a part of the huge legacy he has left Ducati.

'1990 was the year Ducati went forward dramatically. Raymond Roche won the World Superbikes and the new 900SS was introduced. It was the year also that the 888 became a genuine leader in the supersport class. But I felt we should also have a bike which would sell in greater volume. I did not want Ducati to lose its identity in this bike, so I asked the designer Miguel Galluzzi for something which displayed a strong Ducati heritage but which was easy to ride and not a sports bike. He came up with a proposal and I remember seeing the drawings for the first time and I thought, this was the bike Marlon Brando would be riding today in the film *The Wild One!* I was very enthusiastic, it was a great thing and I decided we must produce it.'

The bike was the Monster, the most important bike for Ducati since Bordi's own 851 as it was exactly the volume seller the company needed to stand a chance of real profitability. Bordi had seen the need for it, he had asked for it, it was his decision to make it and he was the one who put the bike into production. Bordi was entirely responsible for the Supermono single-cylinder race bike with its brilliantly innovative slave conrod counter-balance system – his invention. Little

The amiable face of the man behind the most outstandingly successful motorcycle engine of the last 20 years. (Kevin Ash)

investment was needed as it used 888 crankcases and other parts and it was enormously successful. Originally it was intended just as a race bike, but after the TPG takeover Bordi had an idea: 'I thought we could make an air-cooled, naked entry level Ducati from this. It would be priced low enough to compete with scooters, but still be a Ducati.' A Ducati scooter competitor but not a scooter, just as the Monster is a cruiser competitor but not a cruiser... Maybe Bordi would even have produced an automatic transmission for it – he's faced far bigger challenges.

And here we begin to come to the reason why Massimo Bordi, the man who stepped into the legendary Fabio Taglioni's shoes and who went on, arguably, to have as much or an even greater influence on the company, left Ducati in early 2001. 'When the Texas Pacific Group bought Ducati in 1996 everything was very positive,' he says. 'Ducati was a company with very great potential, but it was the only profitable company within a larger group and the funds always went elsewhere, so this potential was never realised. But with TPG came a new era with big resources, and we could reinvest Ducati's own profits back into the company. But we lost something too. The Castiglionis always used to have full confidence in my judgement alone. Now a decision has to be supported by market research, but that way the Monster would never have happened – there was nothing like it you could research!'

So Bordi moved from having the freedom to carry through his ideas but no resources to do it, into the reverse situation – money for new ideas but now with restrictions on what he could do. 'The problem is TPG uses the conventional marketing approach which you do for ordinary products. There's no heart in the decisions any more – it would have meant no Monster, no 851, in the past. Ducati needs a different approach – we're not a mass producer of ordinary goods. This conventional approach actually carries a bigger risk of making mistakes. To make a Ducati you need to understand what the customers might want and not just go by marketing figures. In this I was in conflict with TPG, which is why in the end I could not stay.'

And so Massimo Bordi's career has come full circle – he is now Chief Executive Officer of the Same Deutz-Fahr Group, *diesel* tractor manufacturer and a company some three times larger than Ducati. He's happy enough there. But if a chance arose to return to Ducati? 'Who knows...'

Through Claudio Castiglioni and his brother Gianfranco, Ducati can trace a direct link to the one other motorcycle company which many say comes closest to evoking the same sort of emotions as the Bologna concern: Harley-Davidson. The story begins with aircraft manufacturer Aermacchi, which became well known in the 1950s for a series of single-cylinder racing bikes. Aermacchi's factory on the shores of Lago di Varese was taken over by Harley in 1960 as part of a plan by the Americans to break into the small utility bike market. This was never a great success, especially with unlikely wearers of the Harley name such as the Breeza scooter coming out of the factory, although the Harley-badged two-stroke race bikes fared far better, taking Walter Villa to one 350cc and three 250cc grands prix championships from 1974 to 1976.

The two-stroke road bikes sold reasonably well in the USA in the early 1970s, but eventually they fell foul – literally – of anti-pollution legislation, at the same time as Harley was re-establishing its big V-twins. So Harley-Davidson decided to pull out of Italy.

Meanwhile, Claudio Castiglioni and his brother Gianfranco were successfully running a business making locks, fasteners and some electrical goods, but for both, and especially Claudio, the real passion in their lives came from motorcycles. They found out about the sale, came to an agreement with Harley and in July 1978 bought the factory, where they established a brand new motorcycle company called Cagiva (the name coming from Claudio, Gianfranco and Varese).

Initially they simply rebadged the Harleys as Cagivas, but their own designs followed and were reasonably successful, with production reaching around 40,000 per year. But Claudio wanted to produce bigger bikes – these were where the excitement lie, and although profits were greater on larger machines too, it was the idea of producing proper, big capacity motorcycles which appealed the most.

So he and his brother entered talks with Ducati in 1984 with a view to supplying Ducati engines for Cagiva motorcycles. In the original agreement it was stated that production of complete Ducati motorcycles would cease anyway by the end of 1984, as it was thought the company could be sustained on the Cagiva contract alone. But big Cagiva sales were disappointing – Claudio was discovering the difficulty of marketing a new brand against the

Claudio Castiglioni points the way to a brighter future for motorcycling, reviving the great names. (Motor Cycle News)

The owners with
a passion for their products

Without Castiglioni, the most recognised, beautiful and successful modern motorcycle wouldn't have been built. (Ian Falloon)

established ones. Instead of wading against the flow this way he turned with it, and in 1985 the Castiglionis bought Ducati from the government ownership, with promises to massively increase investment and maintain the production of Ducati motorcycles.

To this day, you'll barely hear a single word from anyone in the factory at any level spoken against Claudio Castiglioni, who is seen, quite simply, as the saviour of Ducati, even though in later years there were once again many financial difficulties. There is very little doubt that without his enthusiasm for motorcycles and for Ducati itself, the Bologna factory would have closed down entirely that year.

With Ducati acquired, a deal incidentally brokered by Romano Prodi, now president of the EU, Castiglioni had no choice but to pour money into Ducati. The old bevel-driven camshaft engines were way past their shelf life while the newer Pantah was in urgent need of development. The company was making big losses and there were no new models imminent.

But he was hooked, his passion for motorcycles in general now focused on one of the great marques, and it was his own! He commissioned Massimo Tamburini first to come up with an interim chassis for the old engines, and although this project was abandoned, was so impressed by him, he took him on to head Cagiva's research and development, where the two men together conceived a host of new motorcycles. The first of these was the radical Paso, essentially a 750 Pantah engine in fully enclosed bodywork with an all-new chassis.

With the Paso and the 906 which was developed from it, Castiglioni was not so much taking Ducati away from the single-minded sports bikes it had been producing as adding to the range, although it wasn't entirely successful as these bikes were never great sellers. But it paved the way in altering the mindset of Ducati fans and other motorcyclists too in thinking of Ducati motorcycles in broader terms, which was exactly what was needed in later years as the markets changed to encompass a greater diversity of machines. The ST2 of 1997 for example was often cited as the spiritual successor to the Paso, and therefore not seen as the first sports-tourer made by Ducati, which certainly eased its entry into the market place.

However, Castiglioni's attempt to expand into the American market was completely misguided.

The Indiana cruiser was a flop even in the USA, while many European and Asian importers refused even to bring the bike in, finding the idea of custom bikes with a desmodromic Ducati engine quite ludicrous.

If Castiglioni was on the one hand trying to break new ground, he wasn't neglecting the traditional Ducati markets, understanding as an enthusiast himself the importance of linking new bikes with the past. So the 750 Sport was introduced, in itself not a great success but which harked back to the 750SS and which was developed into the 900SS, reviving the famous older badge and returning to the Ducati values of minimal weight and simplicity.

On the high performance side, it was thanks to Castiglioni that the eight-valve 851 superbike development surged ahead, the bike which led directly to the 888 and then the 916 and its derivatives, with their world-beating performance matched to the look which has come to define Ducati during the 1990s. This was the machine on which Ducati's reputation today has been built, for all the great machines further back in its past, and it's the bike which has restored credibility to the V-twin as a viable race engine after the world had become convinced only four-cylinder motors could be competitive – so much so that even Honda gave up on its V-fours to follow Ducati's V-twin lead. And it's entirely due to Castiglioni facilitating the work of Bordi, Mengoli and Tamburini that this is the case.

But Castiglioni has another legacy he's left with Ducati. If the SS series represented a link with the past and the eight-valve bikes the way forward, it was the dramatically different and extraordinarily clever M900 Monster and its multiplicity of derivatives which generated the bulk of Ducati's income for much of the 1990s.

The bike was designed by Argentinian Miguel Galluzzi, again with Castiglioni behind him, and although it was mostly an amalgam of existing components – 888 frame, 900SS engine – it created a whole new category of modernist street bike. Here was the cruiser Castiglioni had been searching for – a leisure-oriented town bike yet unmistakably a Ducati.

Like many great enthusiasts, Castiglioni's business sense tended to come second. His enormous passion for racing eventually had Ducati competing in World Superbikes, sometimes with three

teams, while the Cagiva badge was used on an enormously expensive 500 grand prix effort, which after many years very nearly led to race success but at a massive cost.

Effectively all of this racing and the expense it entailed was being paid for solely by Ducati sales. Little sponsorship was garnered for any of the teams as Castiglioni preferred to see his bikes in the factory colours, and there weren't even any Cagiva road models which could be sold on the back of the grand prix effort. Cagiva sales generally were dismal. Ducati simply could not afford it, by 1996 suppliers weren't being paid, parts started to dry up, and when the 916 should have been making record sales figures you couldn't even buy one because production was so erratic. Inevitably, the Castiglionis had to sell Ducati, but the immensely tough negotiating stance they took – as described in this book by Federico Minoli – was a reflection not of their business acumen, but of their desperate reluctance to let go of what had become their life's passion.

Everyone at Ducati recognises this, and Claudio Castiglioni and his brother Gianfranco deserve huge respect for it. It's a cycle the Castiglioni brothers have since repeated with uncanny accuracy. In the mid-1990s they acquired the rights to another famous Italian name, MV Agusta. Their fabulous vision was of a Cagiva Group stable producing Ducati-badged twin-cylinder machines to be sold alongside four-cylinder MV Agustas as well as lower priced Cagivas and Husqvarna off-road machines. It was potentially a force with the breadth to take on the Japanese, but while there was no doubting the concept, much of the business detail was glossed over. The Ducati sale funded development of the Tamburini-designed MV F4, but production of this was faltering by the new millennium and the company became involved in a take-over by the Piaggio scooter group.

Always doing deals or mixing with the famous, Castiglioni manages both with Barry Sheene. Milan, 2001. (*Motor*, Holland)

It's all very well picking out famous names from Ducati's history, or selecting those with the most direct involvement in designing, testing and building the bikes, but what do you find in less obvious areas? In a search for the essence of the passion for Ducati, perhaps it's easier to look for places where it doesn't exist, at people whose involvement is less direct and who might be just as happy doing the same job in an environment producing far less evocative goods. An administrative position, perhaps, where the output is maths rather than machinery, where the job would be the same if the factory were making milk bottles, not motorcycles?

Someone such as Anna Maria Cazzato would be a good person with which to start. Maria is slender, dark and elegant in the highly attractive way of so many Italian women, an appeal she enhances with the natural Mediterranean knack for dressing tastefully and to her strengths. She's also warm, friendly and smiles easily in her office, the manner of someone at ease with her job. Yet potentially it could be both stressful and unrewarding. It turns out to be hard work, certainly – she's an administrative director whose job includes collating and packaging financial information for investors, dealing with legal matters and almost anything else which crops up in the administrative aspects of running just about any factory.

Yet she enjoys the work for its own sake, and not because the paperwork has the 'Ducati' logo at the top. 'I'm always interested in the results which I come up with and it makes me happy if they show there has been some growth.' But the letterhead does help... 'Of course, I follow the racing too. Everyone here does, you just couldn't help getting involved. It's the most important aspect of Ducati. Joining in with all that is completely natural here, it's because we're all a part of the Ducati family.'

So much for searching out someone with no particular feelings for Ducati... Anna Maria even rides one, although she admits it's partly because the company recently had a drive to get more of its women employees on to motorcycles, and she has no illusions about her skill level: 'When I first tried to ride a motorcycle, it was with one of Ducati's test riders. I realised straight away I wasn't ever going to become the next Carl Fogarty! But I passed my test and now I ride my motorcycle regularly, a Monster Dark.' The programme to get more of Ducati's female employees onto

Maybe it's Anna Maria Cazzato's number skills which help her relate to machines like the 998 and M900. (Kevin Ash)

The administrative director
who believes in the soul of Ducati

motorcycles was instigated by the Americans in order to generate a greater sense of involvement, and there has been universal praise for the idea. Anna Maria might only have recently taken to two wheels herself, but her connections with them date back before she started with Ducati in 1994, as she was working at the scooter engine manufacturer Franco Morini. When she decided to change her job, there were plenty of others available, but she chose Ducati. 'When you live in Bologna, you really have to work at Ducati if you possibly can!' she explains. She describes the atmosphere at the factory as quite different to anywhere else. 'My husband Stefano is a technical consultant and he really likes motorcycles, but he works in a different world and doesn't understand what happens here and what it is like. There is such a different way of working at Ducati – although it's a big company there is such a good relationship between all the people, it's still the same atmosphere as a small family concern.

'It does make it very difficult to leave your job here though! Other places just aren't the same, and the money stops being very important when everything else is so good. I know people always say this sort of thing but I really mean it!' The sparkle in her eyes as she says this underlines her sincerity – if you want to employ Anna Maria Cazzato you'll need to do more than wave banknotes under her nose to lure her away from Ducati.

The friendliness within the factory is part of the attraction, but there's more to it. 'There's a really dynamic atmosphere, now so more than ever. There always seems to be something going on, people coming up with new ideas and initiatives. It's very invigorating.'

It's also become a lot better for Anna Maria since the Americans took control of the company.

Ask Anna Maria if she'd be tempted to take a job anywhere else – she'll just laugh and wave you away. (Kevin Ash)

She's seen and been subjected to some of the changes which haven't been obvious to outsiders or observers just of the motorcycles themselves. 'Before the Texas Pacific Group installed its own management, I was dealing with smaller amounts of data and leaving longer periods in between the sets of figures. I often got the impression that all the work I was doing wasn't really being looked at properly or having any real effect.

'The Americans have had a big impact as far as I'm concerned. I've seen it in all the areas I deal with, such as the materials used, the way the management works and the marketing as well. It's completely changed my job. I think there were only about 30 computers in the whole factory before then. Now they're everywhere!' Now Anna Maria is reporting and correlating far more information, doing it more regularly and finding that it's being very carefully looked at. 'It's a lot more satisfying – it's made me feel that my job has become more worthwhile.'

Ducati clearly thinks so too – Anna Maria is the first woman ever at the Borgo Panigale factory to be promoted to a full management position. Did she find she had to be better than the men to get to that position? 'Not especially so. There are always some men who look down on you for being a women, but there are plenty more who treat you as an equal and judge you by the job you do, not what sex you are. Anyway, the pay is the same!' Maybe so, but with her increased workload and the responsibility of her job, Anna Maria certainly works long hours, finishing only when she's decided the job is done rather than when the clock says it's time to go home. 'I don't really mind this as I like doing things properly and by myself. I don't have any children either, which makes a difference. But it has helped that in the last few years I have felt more valued.'

She has no doubt that there's something special about Ducati – that's why you'll see her at events such as the World Ducati Weekend or watching the Superbike racing on television – but it's not easily defined. 'There is a soul perhaps, or a desire here, but I don't really know. It's something intangible, and perhaps that's why it's so precious.' But she might have touched upon a clue inadvertently when we were talking about some of her personal background, such as her marriage in 1990. 'I was working for Morini at the time, not Ducati, but Taglioni was acting as a consultant for the firm. And he sent me a white orchid. I was very moved by that. He really is a great man.'

Passion is not a word you'd associate with Chris Clarke. He's straight talking, sometimes blunt and generally, by his own admission, rather cynical. But as owner of one of the UK's older Ducati dealerships still with the marque, he's certainly lived through some 'interesting' times, since he took on the franchise in 1979. There have been plenty of positive noises coming out of the factory since the late 1990s, the excited talk of fresh new faces with big ideas and commitments for the future, and many other people have been caught up in it. Even Clarke in fact isn't as dismissive as those who know him might have expected. Nevertheless, he has seen and heard it all before, and in the past, eventually Ducati has headed downwards again after a burst of enthusiasm, so a little world-weariness is understandable.

His involvement with motorcycling was almost inevitable as his father was a speedway rider, serving many years with the Norwich Stars, so Chris was brought up with bikes, riding old British machines such as a 350 Velocette. At 16 he began trials riding, and in 1975 moved into the motorcycle business proper by starting up his dealership. Four years later he'd become a Ducati outlet. 'The bikes in those days were great! They were always exclusive but they were very successful in racing. I remember in the Avon Tyres Production race series it was always the 900SS up against the Moto Guzzi Le Mans and the Laverda Jota. The Japanese bikes were more powerful but they just didn't handle as well, and these were the three bikes to have.' Fine to race then, but what was the dealer's view? 'There did seem to be rather a lot of PDI to do!' PDI is the pre-delivery inspection, where the dealer takes the bike from the crate as it's delivered and builds it up into a machine which is ready for the customer. 'The hardest thing was balancing the carburettors, especially on those bikes which had a separate throttle cable for each carb.

'Ducati definitely had some bad problems at that time, all sorts of things would fail... cranks, gearboxes and so on. The bikes were really nice to ride, but they took an awful lot of looking after. That part of it's changed today, the quality is far better and they don't need so much attention. But they're still exclusive, and then as now, they're the bikes everyone aspires to.'

The factory's problems in the early 1980s didn't get in the way of Clarke as much as he might have expected as bike supply was not really a problem, although he wasn't asking for very many –

Chris Clarke has seen it all with Ducati: ownership changes, supply and quality problems. He's still with them! (Kevin Ash)

The **dealer** who
remains **fired** up after 22 years

not enough to have kept his business going if he had been a sole franchise. It was more the direction the bikes themselves were going in which he didn't like so much: 'I think it started to go awry with the 900 S2 – that came in some nasty colours, and the power was badly affected by the big Silentium silencers, as well as the sound. The bikes were becoming messed up when they had to comply with emissions laws.' The quality fell to an all-time low by 1985 too, although it was patchy rather than consistently bad. Clarke says that while some bikes were constantly in and out of his workshops to have all sorts of problems sorted – gearbox and crankshaft failures, electrical troubles, poor quality paint and so on – others were fine and seemed to go on forever without any trouble. 'I thought it was funny that Ducati put a leaded seal on the crankcase, so you could tell if anyone had opened the engine up. It became quite a thing to have a high mileage engine with its seal still intact!'

Sales started to pick up with the arrival of the Paso then the 851, although the first example, the Tricolore in 1988 was hard to get – Clarke saw very few of those. He thinks that's a shame: 'I loved those carefully reversed cone silencers, they sounded good, and reliability wasn't really a problem either.' The real volume sales didn't start until 1989 with the arrival of the red 851: 'People talk about them having problems but we found they were really good. The only trouble I remember was vaporisation in the fuel lines when the bikes were used in traffic on hot days. But that was about it. It was amazing they could produce a bike like that at all, a company which had been in that dreadful state. Then the wins started coming in Superbike racing, and that boosted sales right across the range, the new SS in 1990 doing well along with the 851, then 888. The

Sometimes you wonder if Clarke is a little sad at seeing one of his bikes go. He's not – this is his business. (Kevin Ash)

bikes were still very expensive but they'd never lost that aspirational quality.' The 1990s proved to be the real turning point: 'The new look 900SS in 1991 sold better, and this was the beginning of decent sales of Ducatis. It looked better, but the real difference was that all of the old problems on the previous model were completely sorted. It now had a pair of Mikuni carburettors instead of that silly Weber twin-choke carb, the steering had been sharpened up, Japanese Showa suspension was fitted which was far superior to the old stuff ... they'd taken every single criticism on board and put it right for that model.' In 1993 the first Monster 900s started arriving. These sold reasonably well, but were never as big as they were in some other European countries. 'The SS was still a bigger seller for me,' says Clarke. Then at the end of that year he went to the motorcycle show at the NEC in Birmingham. 'I saw the 916 for the first time – it was just fantastic! So many things came together at the right time for that bike, it's so improbable really. Bordi's engine was getting better and better, while Tamburini was the great stylist, and the engineers made it perform well enough to do so well in World Superbikes. Everyone's lifetime best ideas, all in the one machine!

'Absolutely outstanding ... and then you couldn't get any! In the years that followed you had to wait months and months for them, and even then you'd only get a handful of bikes. I could have sold loads more than we did. Nothing arrived on time, promises were broken, and we had a few problems with the bikes, such as regulators, sidestands falling off, the clutch gave us difficulties. Anything that took money to solve was just left, but if it could be fixed cheaply they sorted it. The clutch was made much better after they started assembling them differently!'

Then the Americans took over: 'Things got much better for us in 1997 – bikes turned up, the numbers were up and we started to get more interesting models, such as the 955SP. I haven't been entirely happy about the MHe900 being sold solely on the internet, but the general feeling is that it's all beginning to work very well.

'I do believe Ducati now is in serious danger of getting it right!' And as he says this, it's hard to ignore the impression that Chris Clarke the no-nonsense businessman has a spark in his eyes. He's far too English to describe as passionate, but there's no hiding it – he's rather fired up!

If you read a chronological story of Ducati the name Franco Farnè will crop up very early on, even before the arrival of Fabio Taglioni at the Bologna factory. Continue through the history, from Ducati's early race successes at the Motogiro, into the 1960s competition efforts and up to the epochal Imola 200 victory of Paul Smart; keep going to Hailwood's famous Isle of Man win in 1978, follow the development of Bordi's eight-valve twins, the arrival of the 916, Fogarty's four World Superbike Championships, until, half a century of history later, you might be learning about the semi-works Ducati NCR Superbike race team. And throughout, at so many of the pivotal, memorable moments, somewhere you will see the name of Franco Farnè.

'At first I was working on bikes like the Cucciolo and the Cruiser, which didn't go well unfortunately. Then I began racing, and I rode in the first Motogiro with the Cucciolo. I didn't make it to the end and stopped in the second leg. Other Ducati racers on this occasion included Alberto Farnè, but he was not related to me, as many people think. He was much older – I was just a kid!' I did the second Giro with the 98GT and then the following year on the 98 Sport where I came about tenth on both occasions. I also did it with the Marianna, when there were 40 racers including Spaggiari, Villa, Degli Antoni. I was ninth. The last year I did it on the 100 desmo. It was a unique bike, the only one. Spaggiari and Ganduzzi were on 125s. Unfortunately, in the second race I had problems and Montano asked me to bring the bike back to Bologna, so that was the last Giro I did.' Farnè breaks off at this point to scold NCR rider Brock Parkes for strolling about in only his underpants – we're sitting in the NCR hospitality tent at the Brands Hatch World Superbike round – but his humour wins out in the end: 'That's obscene! Still, he made some good times today, so we'll let him off.'

Farnè has no doubt about who made Ducati what it is today. 'When Fabio Taglioni arrived in 1954 there was a great deal of change. Prior to that everything had been based around the Cucciolo mostly, but then there were many new and great bikes. Taglioni was the magic of Ducati. Later on he didn't believe in the eight-valve engine, and of course this has been an amazing success, but he was without a doubt the essence of Ducati. On hearing about his death I was deeply saddened. I sent a telegram saying he was the greatest engineer I have ever known. He

In half a century Franco Farnè, on Mike Hailwood's left, has worked with all of Ducati's greatest riders. (Mick Woollett)

The race mechanic who couldn't
give up even after he retired

taught me everything, not just at work but also in life. He was a true Romagnolo – genuine to the core and really spontaneous. He knew me affectionately as the mouse because I was small, and he used to take time out to show me how to do things in the technical sense rather than, like so many others would, go for the easy option and say I couldn't do that and then give the task to someone else.'

Today, Farnè gives the impression that he feels Ducati might be losing something as it strives to come to terms with the economic realities of the modern world. In this he agrees with Massimo Bordi, a man with whom Farnè says he worked very well. 'Ducati today is creating an industrial factory whereas in my day it was still very much artisan-based, even though it employed many people. The fact is, even if the Japanese are great at developing new technology, we Italians are still able to come up with innovative ideas. It's in our blood. Also we have always worked towards an end result regardless of time. If it meant working all night that's what we did, even if we might have complained a little! Ducati for me has remained one of the most important companies in Italy. It has always produced highly skilled and creative workers, whether they use their heads or their hands.'

Farnè's passion was one of the crucial factors in maintaining the company's race effort in the 1970s. At this time Ducati had come under the control of the government-owned EFIM Group, which was more interested in cold economics than what it saw as the indulgence of the race effort. An inner circle driven by Taglioni and Farnè worked together with the Scuderia NCR team formed by ex-Ducati race mechanics Giorgio Nepoti and Rino Caracchi (Nepoti, Caracchi Racing gives NCR its initials) to form a race shop which was partially independent of the factory – enough so for the

Farnè in retirement and no pipe or slippers in sight. Donington, 2001, in the Ducati NCR pit garage. (Kevin Ash)

EFIM accountants to miss exactly what was going on. The NCR team, now with Farnè as a pivotal member, produced V-twins to compete in the endurance and Formula 1 classes, precipitating the Ducati tradition of making highly-competitive race machines available for general sale. The pinnacle of NCR's achievement at that time was Mike Hailwood's 1978 TT win. Although the team's main involvement was in supplying the bike, which was subsequently prepared by Steve Wynne's Sports Motorcycles, without the men of NCR Hailwood's Ducati comeback would not have happened and it's no exaggeration to say that Ducati's history would look very different today. Farnè was one of the two mechanics sent over to work on Hailwood's bike. There could be no-one with more experience – he had helped develop, prepare and maintain the 750SS on which Paul Smart took that amazing first place at Imola in 1972. Farnè had huge respect for Hailwood: 'I spent a lot of time in England working on Hailwood's 900SS so I got to know him well. He was not just a great racer, but a great man as well.'

During the 1980s and well into the 1990s Farnè was still deeply involved in the development of Ducati's race machines, and it wasn't until 1996, at the age of 62, and with his entire working life spent at Ducati, that he finally decided it was time to retire. 'But I just couldn't stop working! So I continued at Ducati on a semi-retired basis until Bimota offered me a very interesting project working on its new World Superbike machine. We did very well considering we only worked on it for two and a half months. We even won a race in that time with Gobert in Australia.'

After the collapse of Bimota through severe financial difficulties Farnè still couldn't bring himself to retire properly and he returned to Ducati and the NCR race team, which surely has him to thank for its very existence today. 'My wife has always supported me throughout my career. She would come to race meetings and never complain, even though before a race I didn't want her there! I used to shut myself off and become totally focused on the race ahead. And she has always defended my role at Ducati. When a journalist insinuated that Ducati had sent me to Bimota to get rid of me, she made sure in very strong terms that he stood corrected!'

What an absurd implication that would be. Here was a man who had dedicated his entire life to the Ducati cause, an embodiment of the very heart of the marque. Far from trying to get rid of Farnè, Ducati should reserve a special position in its museum for him!

C arl Fogarty is the most successful racer in the history of the World Superbike series. He has more pole positions, more race wins and of course – with four titles – more championships than any other rider. His achievements were already hugely impressive before Superbikes, including Isle of Man TT victories (coming with a lap record which lasted seven years), the TT Formula 1 world title and the World Endurance Championship. And this last title was almost an aside, a paid ride which Fogarty took up solely to fund his prime goal, to compete in the World Superbike Championship.

Despite retirement from racing in 2000 after breaking his left arm severely in a crash in Australia, Fogarty remains the most popular, high-profile British rider since Barry Sheene in the 1970s and early 1980s. Foggy alone was responsible for reviving his countrymen's interest in motorcycle racing which was flagging desperately when it seemed that only American or Australian riders had the background and backing to make it at the very highest level.

He was one of the main reasons why World Superbikes forged ahead of the blue riband grand prix racing in popularity in the UK, a fact driven home when at the WSB round at Brands Hatch in 1999 the record 120,000 crowd was even bigger than the numbers attending the Formula One car grand prix at Silverstone (or even who would have attended had the car parks not been flooded). Indeed, in attendance terms it was the biggest sporting event of any description in Britain that year. In comparison the motorcycle grand prix at Donington couldn't attract close to 30,000 through its gates.

Fogarty's appeal was muted to begin with. He never looked comfortable in front of TV cameras or giving interviews, although journalists quickly realised he was also not afraid of speaking his mind, caring little for the political consequences.

The Blackburn lad had plenty of help getting started – his father, ex-racer George Fogarty, was enormously supportive in the early stages. But it was Carl's talent which took him off from there, his extraordinary ability to make a motorcycle go around a race track faster than anyone else.

There was another factor, as the many interviews and books about him have always concluded – he simply could not stand to lose. To Fogarty, coming second was just as much of a failure as

Four times World Superbike Champion Carl Fogarty's chilling stare is as memorable as his riding style. (Kel Edge)

King **Carl** the Ducati champion who couldn't **bear** to lose

finishing last. It wasn't winning, it wasn't proving to himself as much as to anyone else that he was the best, fastest man out there.

In 1991, therefore, he was not having a good time. He was campaigning in World Superbikes as a Honda UK rider on an ageing RC30, a once great bike which was now comprehensively outpaced, and being run not by the factory but by the British importer, inevitably with fewer resources than the major concerns, even though it was always one of the top teams.

Fogarty still managed to finish as the top Honda rider in seventh position overall, ahead even of former champion Fred Merkel. But it had meant pushing his bike to the very ragged edge for, at best, a top six result, which is as mentally punishing for a rider with his consuming drive to win as it was limiting to a career. He also had recurring handling problems, specifically with the front tyre sliding away in mid-corner, no matter what the team did with the bike's geometry, suspension or tyres. It was a handling trait which caused many other riders to fall off their RC30s, but the way Fogarty coped underlined the exceptional nature of his skill.

Without any sense of trying to impress (as if he needed to) or that it might be something unusual, he explained: 'The front end was always going on that bike. What I'd do was hold it up on my knee until the tyre gripped again, but by then it had run wide.' Run wide maybe, but where other riders were regularly coming to grief, Fogarty was staying on the bike and crossing the finishing line intact. This was the last season that Honda UK would campaign the RC30 in World Superbikes, but come 1992 and Fogarty turned his back on the traditional and easy option of

If Fogarty had a weakness it was wet weather races. Here his 888 leads at Brands moments before he fell off. (Don Morley)

pursuing the backwater which was a British Championship career, choosing instead to race at the highest level he could, in World Superbikes. This he could only fund privately, paying for it partly with savings and partly by riding for Kawasaki in the World Endurance series.

The bike he bought for WSB was a Ducati 888, and there's one very pragmatic reason behind this decision. He needed a competitive machine, and with his mental attitude he needed what was unequivocally the best bike he could possibly buy. There was no choice, but that's not a euphemism for suggesting the Ducati was the best bike out there: quite simply, the 888 was all he could get! 'I really don't know how Ducati does it,' he says now. 'Here's this small Italian factory against the big Japanese guys, yet it's the only one you can buy a race bike from which is good enough to win a World Championship! Why don't the others do that? I can't understand it. In 1992 Kawasaki was strong in World Superbikes and so was Yamaha, but you couldn't buy bikes like those the factory was running. Ducati would sell you a machine which was on the pace when it came out of the box!'

This was a time when the manufacturers were making machines available to the public which had certain features they wanted to use on their World Superbike racers. The rules stated that the race bikes had to share many technical characteristics with their showroom road bike equivalents, so limited editions of some machines were produced purely to comply with the rules. Going on to make those machines into truly competitive race bikes demanded huge additional expenses to buy comprehensive factory race kits – if you could get them in the first place – and you'd still need to have specialist tuning work carried out.

But the Ducati 888 you bought, then you raced it in World Superbikes. 'When the bike arrived I asked where all the lights were and stuff,' says Fogarty. 'On the other bikes you even had to convert them from road specification, but the Ducati arrived ready to put on the track. If Kawasaki had done the same thing then, my career could have been completely different, but it was only with the Ducati that I stood a chance of doing well.'

Fogarty and the 888 were well matched – his wayward front end problems were banished at a stroke – but after finishing twelfth in the first round in Spain in pouring rain, disastrously he

Fogarty never hid his
feelings, endearing himself
to many and alienating
others with his ripe
opinions. (Gold & Goose)

crashed while leading at Donington. World Superbike rounds each comprise two races, and it's this 'second chance' option which in retrospect could well have been pivotal to Fogarty's career. In race two Fogarty again took the lead, but this time he maintained his position to the end, breaking the lap record on the way and proving both his own breathtaking talent and Ducati's unique ability, and its will, to 'productionise' its World Superbike contenders.

Fogarty might have bought a Ducati for 1992, but Ducati returned the compliment by buying Fogarty, signing him up for the works team. The Lancashire rider had had an amazing season in which he broke the Isle of Man TT lap record on a Yamaha, rode an astonishing race in the British 500cc Grand Prix on an uncompetitive privateer bike (only to be felled by an oil spill when in sixth spot), along with winning that World Endurance Championship – and, of course, getting a WSB home victory at Donington, from pole.

Yet the chance of a factory ride looked like eluding him in this pervading atmosphere which suggested only Americans or Australians could win world titles, especially in grands prix. But a call did come, from ex-superbike champion Raymond Roche, who was to be Ducati's team manager in 1993. And so the symbiotic relationship between Fogarty and Ducati began in earnest. Fogarty went on to win World Superbike championships – in 1994, 1995, 1998 and 1999 – breaking his relationship with the Italians just the once in 1996 when he was tempted back to Honda to ride an RC45 for the factory team, based in Louth in the UK.

This was Fogarty's worst ever year as a factory superbike rider. He finished fourth overall, proving again that his riding style, which depended on very high cornering speeds and extreme lean angles, was better suited to the Ducati 916 and its race derivatives, where the Honda demanded that corners be 'squared off' and the bike pulled upright as soon as possible for the screaming high rev power delivery to work at its best.

But the differences extended way beyond the behaviour of the bikes. Fogarty also seemed to suffer from culture shock. 'I always felt very much that at Honda I was just another fish in the sea. Ducati is the only factory racing where the boss of the company will drop in to the pit garage for a chat or a drink, and who'll come up on the podium with you when you win. He's as proud as you are! At Honda, I didn't even know the name of the factory boss, let alone meet him!'

Ducati was like a big family to Fogarty, happy to accept both him and his favourite race mechanic Anthony 'Slick' Bass (who was fired by Honda almost as soon as the 1996 season started) and his wife Michaela – see her foreword! Ducati ran a small, tight-knit team, but this had a relaxed and relatively easy-going atmosphere that suited Fogarty much better than the intense, scheduled, corporate approach of Honda. He recognised something else in Ducati. 'Ducati is different, definitely. Obviously the bike was the only V-twin when everyone else was running fours, which all looked the same too. But the bikes handle so well, they have those classic looks and bright red colour – it's the same thing as Ferrari.'

For someone in Fogarty's position there can of course be a downside to riding an icon. The passion for 'Ducati the motorcycle brand' can usurp the achievements of the riders – it's something the boss of the rival Aprilia factory, Ivano Beggio, once complained about as his aim was to maximise the profile of Aprilia. His company's fabulous successes in the smaller grand prix classes were inevitably headlined as 'Max Biaggi wins...' while the simultaneous achievements of Fogarty so often were hailed as Ducati victories.

Aprilia's disadvantage will take time to correct, simply because time is the missing ingredient. Ducati has a motorcycling history which goes back half a century and has taken its fans through all the highs and lows you'd expect over such a period, endearing many and alienating some in the process. As a serious sports motorcycle manufacturer Aprilia is barely out of nappies in comparison, and it can only wait to accrue its history.

Fogarty hinted at this in his early days as a factory Ducati rider, a little disconcerted at how the balance of exposure – even after his first World Superbike title – seemed tilted towards the marque and away from the man. But today he doesn't think that at all. Ducati feels to him much as it looks from the outside, his natural home.

It's why he's staying with Ducati after retiring from racing: 'I'm still involved doing promotional stuff, helping with the race school and so on. I don't have any long-term plans so I'll keep doing this for a while and my commentary with the BBC – I think I'm busier now than I ever was when I

was racing! 'Funnily enough I don't miss the racing as much as I thought I would. Yes, I do miss that feeling you get when you've won a race and you're standing at the top of a podium, but it's not been as bad as I expected.

'I was disappointed in the way it all ended, being forced to stop near the beginning of the season because of injury. But in a way the timing wasn't bad – the mid-30s is when racers start to retire anyway, so it hasn't cut my career very short. And it could have been a lot worse!'

Carl Fogarty's interest in the racing scene hasn't waned one bit since retirement. He's currently keeping a very keen eye on the progress of Ruben Xaus, who some see as a sort of protégé of his. He doesn't quite view it like that: 'We were just good mates really, from 1999 onwards. I saw he was very fast then and encouraged Ducati to sign him in 2000 and again for the 2001 season. We used to enjoy winding him up. I'd take the piss and tell him he was slow, and it just made him go faster. He's often said he wants to be like me. He really wants to win, and he's fast and brave too.'

At the end of the 2001 season Xaus showed Fogarty's and Ducati's faith in him was well placed, winning races by setting a pace just too hot for the rest of the field. In interviews afterwards Xaus has made a point of praising Fogarty for his help. Ducati too appreciates Fogarty's input – since his retirement from competition it's offered him a longer contract to work as an ambassador than any he signed to race for the company.

This is such a deep-rooted relationship. Even during Fogarty's year with Castrol Honda, most of his fans would still be wearing Ducati logos alongside their Foggy badges.

Fogarty's link with Ducati continued when his racing had stopped – he became an ambassador. (Gold & Goose)

Paul Smart's famous win in 1972 on the Ducati 750 V-twin ahead of Giacomo Agostini and a field of top riders on the world's best bikes had influences beyond setting a direction for Ducati's future race effort and splashing the company's name across the motorcycle press around the world. In amongst the 70,000 crowd was a 15-year-old boy by the name of Andrea Forni, on whom this astonishing victory had a profound effect. He recalls it vividly even today: 'It was amazing – Agostini was beaten! This was just so incredible! The crowd there was huge, and they just couldn't believe what was happening in front of them. These two Ducatis were faster and it was astonishing they were so strong.

'This had an enormous influence on me as I wanted to be an engineer even at that age. In Italy anyway 99 per cent of engineers now want to work above all for Ferrari or Ducati. Ducati was not so well known then but after this race I knew I wanted to work for them.'

Forni went on to gain an engineering degree at the University of Bologna while at the same time acquiring some formidable riding skills. He had a motorcycle as soon as he was allowed, getting a rare Chimatti 125 at the age of 16 followed shortly after by a Morini 3½ Sport, then inevitably two Ducatis, even though this was before any direct involvement in the factory. Forni worked initially with the Weber/Magnetti-Marelli carburettor and fuel injection company – a supplier to Ducati – where his job was testing new components and systems in the research and development department rather than the drawing office in which many engineers begin their careers, but he was only there for three years before a vacancy came up at Ducati, in 1988.

The job, in essence, was much the same as at Weber: working in the prototype department developing new designs. The difference was that these were now complete motorcycles, Ducati motorcycles on which the future not just of the factory rested but the hopes, dreams and expectations of enthusiasts worldwide. Forni's job is to turn the ideas, sketches and technical drawings into rideable prototype machines which he then has to develop so they can be produced efficiently and ridden by road riders, or racers. The list of machines he has developed is a list of almost every motorcycle Ducati has produced during the 1990s and into the 21st century, but his favourite is the bike on which Ducati's modern reputation has been built, the 916.

Andrea Forni makes music on a 996R – his studio is the anechoic chamber used to ease the twins through the noise test. (Kevin Ash)

A **development** engineer
who rides his prototypes to the limit

The set-up of every new
Ducati since the 1990s
has been finalised by
Forni, here with a 1998
900SS. (Roland Brown)

'It's difficult to define exactly what is the essence of Ducati,' he says. 'But whatever it is, the 916 has it 100 per cent!' As far as Forni is concerned, it's a combination of factors which makes Ducati special, all to do with a commitment to sport as well as style. For him the 916 is a true sports machine, with a heritage gained from its predecessors and authenticity which comes from its fabulous track successes. And he's very proud of it, rightly, because the 916 is the way it is through Forni's work on developing the bike – remember this is a machine which won the World Superbike Championship in its first year of competition.

The machine he's most fond of after the 916 unsurprisingly is the 888, partly because development of this was more difficult than the 916. 'I think we were working more with the unknown with this bike, pushing technical boundaries more, as it hadn't really been shown that a V-twin could truly compete with the Japanese four-cylinder bikes at that stage. This is why I am also very fond of that bike – it was a major advance in displaying what a V-twin could do.'

A huge amount of effort went into developing the fuel injection system on the 888 as it was very advanced compared with anything else used on motorcycles up to that time, owing more to Formula One car technology than anything else. Making an injection system work is a soul-destroying, time-consuming process – an on-board computer has to store in its memory the correct amount of fuel to inject at every combination of throttle opening and rpm up to the maximum from tickover, and it's Andrea Forni at Ducati who inputs that information. So, at 3,000rpm he has to find the optimum amount of fuel to inject at full throttle for maximum power, then again at a slightly smaller throttle opening, right to the point where the throttle is almost closed. The process must be repeated at 3,100rpm, and in small increments right across the range.

On top of this, the fuel injection system has to compensate for changes in barometric pressure, ambient temperature and a range of other variables which might influence the correct fuel/air mixture. And when he has done this, there's the rest of the bike to worry about! His testing covers every aspect of a machine, right down to whether the switchgear operates with the right feel and reliability. Indeed, it was Forni's opinion of some types of cut-off switches which dictated Ducati's controversial fitment for many years of automatic flip-up sidestands. Where most Japanese production bikes demand that the rider kicks up the sidestand with his heel before riding away, on Ducatis up to the year 2000, as soon as the bike's weight was lifted off the stand it would spring up and out of the way.

It sounds like a good idea, preventing the possibility of riding off with the stand still extended, which has the potential to throw off the rider as soon as he tries to corner to the left. But it also means the stand must be held extended until the bike is leaning on it firmly, and if the pressure should be released for any reason (even a strong gust of wind can do it, or perhaps a stranger interfering with a parked Ducati) it flips up and the bike can fall over. Conspiracy theorists have it that Ducati used these stands in order to sell more spare body parts, but Forni has a more pragmatic explanation: 'To comply with regulations, it must not be possible to ride off with the stand extended. The Japanese achieve this with switches which determine when the stand is extended, when the bike is in neutral and whether the clutch lever is pulled in. If the clutch is being let out with the bike in gear and the stand out, the engine is killed. But the switches we were allowed to use simply weren't reliable enough and would have caused too many problems, especially in wet weather, so instead we came up with the self-retracting sidestand as an engineering solution.

'Anyway, I prefer it! You just lift up the bike and don't have to think about the stand. But now we buy our switches from a Japanese manufacturer and use the same system as everyone else.'

This willingness to find alternative sources for some components is one of the few signs Forni has seen from his department's point of view of the American take-over of Ducati in 1998. 'I think in the first two years there was very little influence in the research and development department – things carried on much as before. The main effort appeared to go into the marketing while we were allowed to keep going as we were, although this might be changing more now, as we are working on new models.'

It's not just Forni's skills as a development engineer which are highly respected at Ducati, it's his ability as a rider which is spoken of in some considerable awe. Yet this blend of riding and technical skills is essential for Forni to carry out his job effectively – in developing a supersports

motorcycle he really needs to be able to ride it to its limits to determine the effect of his changes. What leaves anyone white-faced who has the privilege of following Forni around the demanding, twisting roads around Bologna is the realisation that he exercises his hard riding talents on the roads as much as the race track.

Yet Forni has never raced, learning how to ride while touring (at speed, no doubt...), and he has some serious trips behind him, including a tour to Portugal on his Ducati Pantah 600, after which he took the bike to the infamous Elefant Rally, a gruelling north European winter event in freezing, snowy conditions, known to attract only the hardiest riders. Forni went twice, the second time in 1990 when he decided the rally would be a good test of the prototype 907ie which he was working on. But even he has his limits: 'Twice at the Elefant Rally is enough!' he says.

It's hard to imagine Forni today having enough time for this sort of thing. He works long hours either at the factory, the high-speed testing circuit at Nardo in the south of Italy or out in the sinuous back roads in the hills surrounding Bologna, honing the next generation of Ducati motorcycles. And the hardest thing he has to do is decide when to stop. 'Always the most difficult thing of all is deciding when something is good enough, even though it is not perfect,' he says. 'You could go on and on developing a component until it is absolutely perfect but it would take impossibly long to get a motorcycle into production this way. You must reach a point where you must stop and say, this is good enough. That is hard!'

But seeing Forni's blend of skills and his dedication, it's clear that when he says something is good enough, for most other people that's as close to perfection as you'll ever get.

For Forni's job you need to be a brilliant engineer, an outstanding rider and a perfectionist. That's all.
(Kevin Ash)

Now here's a job title you wouldn't have heard in the Ducati factory before the Americans took control: Luca Francolini is a kaizen facilitator. More conventionally he's also known as an assistant manager in the assembly department, where he works mostly on the faired motorcycle assembly lines, where the superbikes and SS models are made. Like assistant managers the world over, his job seems to involve doing just about anything and everything. 'My responsibilities include following up the daily production numbers, taking care of anything which might interfere with the continuous flow of the production line, making sure the workers are happy and sorting out any problems they might have. And then there's the kaizen...'

Here is a very real indication of how the new management installed by the Texas Pacific Group has been dragging the historic Ducati factory (and for 'historic' read old-fashioned as far as production methods were concerned) into the 21st century. With its relatively small production numbers and labour-intensive assembly Ducati could never expect to compete directly with the Japanese in terms of unit costs, but encumbered as it was with methodology which dated back to the 1960s it's no surprise the company was failing, regardless of the excellence of its products.

Kaizen is a Japanese term, originally coined by Masaaki Imai to describe a process of continuous improvement involving an entire workforce. It's a strategy for getting everyone in a factory or section of a factory to work together in coming up with new ideas for making things better, whether it's to the benefit of production itself or to the working conditions. 'There is a small group of people who are trying to improve the way of thinking at the factory,' says Francolini. 'I do this from the production point of view. And it is happening all the time, even though we have already made many changes – kaizen says that there is no limit to the improvements you can make.

'It's not necessarily in large steps but in the form of small changes, one after the other.'

The changes have had a big effect in more than one way too – the production line off which rolls a relentless stream of 996 superbikes throughout the day is an example. 'A few months ago you would not have recognised this as the same production line!' says Francolini. Those changes can be anything from small details to much more major systems or structural alterations. So you might find the workers simply standing in different positions or at different heights than before, or

The blue boxes of parts found on assembly lines, improving efficiency, were Luca Francolini's brainwave. (Kevin Ash)

Workers put forward really **useful** ideas
says the **kaizen** facilitator

large assembly machinery in a completely different location alongside the line.

One of Francolini's own ideas is the blue plastic box which accompanies each bike on its journey down the line. In it is a selection of components put together in the box beforehand, in a particular order, making them far more convenient for the production line workers than when they were in trays at the side of the line. He's proud of this, and of his kaizen work as a whole: 'I get a great satisfaction from this sort of thing because the workers themselves take part as much as we do, and they are very happy to see how their own ideas go on to help them in their jobs, as well as benefiting the Ducati factory. I can see how over the last year the quality of the bikes has been improving, and that's as a direct result of the work I am doing, which makes me feel very good.

'The workers put forward a lot of ideas, and the good thing is now at Ducati there is a real possibility of changes being made straight away. The young people especially like that. Of course, sometimes mistakes are made, but this is all a part of the process of growing up, for the individuals themselves as people, for them professionally and also for the factory.'

Things were quite different for Francolini before he came to work at Ducati, about a year earlier – he was employed at the Iveco truck factory (a part of the giant Fiat group), where he was working as an engineer in the production department. 'There wasn't the possibility to make any real changes there,' he says. 'It was more a case of constantly having people telling you not to change things!' There was something of a tease in Francolini's life while at Iveco, which makes him laugh now: 'I used to work about 100km from Bologna, and every day I would drive past here and

Whether it's production details or employee wellbeing, Francolini's quest is to make things better. (Kevin Ash)

see the huge poster on the factory wall. Each day I would think how much I wanted to work at Ducati instead!' Seeing as Francolini admits he had no interest in motorcycles at the time, that might seem rather surprising. He couldn't ride a bike and if he had any feelings at all about them, he didn't really like them much! Yet he has made quite a commitment to work here, as both he and his girlfriend plus their respective families all come from Rome, a long way from Bologna. He says the easiest thing for him to do would be to leave Ducati now and return to Rome: 'But I'm not! So my girlfriend instead is having to come up to Bologna to look for a job here.'

Why did he come here? 'Ducati is special. As an engineer I always wanted to work for Ferrari or Ducati, that's how it is in Italy. It's because of the impact the company has, because of its history and the image, and in terms of your career, having worked a spell at Ducati definitely improves your prospects outside.' He's thinking of moving on? 'Definitely not. I am very happy here, and now I am learning to be crazy about motorcycles. Well, Ducati motorcycles... I can ride one now!

'And I like it too much here to move. When I meet people and tell them I work for Ducati, they're always impressed and that's a good feeling. And it's a company with such history and soul.

'I think that comes from many things, but mostly from Taglioni. Before him, Ducati was nothing special, just another little company, but it has grown up with him and because of him. So many things have happened to Ducati over the 75 years of its history, so many difficulties and triumphs, and now we have the big successes in World Superbike racing.'

There's one more thing too, which he says while laughing: 'Oh, and I love the sound of the bikes! I can always tell a Ducati from a long way off, even when I can't see it – the sound of the engine is unique and very special.'

From having no interest in motorcycles Francolini now finds he can't leave them alone: 'I remember once when I went back to Rome for the elections, I saw a Ducati in the street and I waved him down because I wanted to see what he had done to his bike. He'd made some changes to the exhaust system and I was curious, and I just had to have a look!

'Ducati riders are always personalising their bikes – I like that.'

Francolini meanwhile is busy personalising the production line...

D avid Gross, like many Americans, was a dirt bike fan in his youth – sporting road motorcycles were never big in the States and didn't register in his life. He knew of Ducati and that it was a historic company, but not the details of that history. So he went his way, Ducati went its own way and the two seemed unlikely to meet.

Then a relationship, first with Italy, was established when in 1996 as a corporate lawyer in New York, Gross became deeply involved in a deal which involved the Banca Commerciale Italiane. He acquired a working knowledge of Italy and Italians through working and living in the country, and the step into the world of Ducati followed shortly after when the Texas Pacific Group, impressed by his experience and qualifications, asked him to act as a consultant in the deal it was trying to establish in its complex and time-consuming takeover of Ducati.

Gross worked closely with Federico Minoli, Ducati's president today, initially in developing the company, then in the process of taking it public, up to the share flotation on the New York and Milan stock exchanges in March 1999.

The flotation was successful, TPG owns around 35 per cent of Ducati's shares and Gross is fully established at the Bologna factory which employs him full time, his attention now turned to Ducati's marketing and product development. It might hurt many Italians to read this, but the clarity of this American lawyer's understanding of what Ducati means to people (and indeed what people mean to Ducati) has been absolutely pivotal in the revival of the company. The Ducati factory today is a place fair bursting with confidence, warmth, enthusiasm and optimism, and Gross must take a large measure of responsibility for that.

His enthusiasm and energy leave their mark too – an interview with Gross is not so much an exchange of questions and answers, more like opening a floodgate and standing back to watch and listen. It took a simple and obvious question to set him off: why did TPG want to buy Ducati?

'When they found Ducati and realised it was available, it was like finding some great undiscovered jewel! Here was a company which had this amazing product but which was not doing anything with the brand.

'This is perfect for TPG. As a venture capital company it has plenty of experience and it's very

David Gross understood the world's motorcycle markets and saw a demand for the 2003 Multistrada. (Kevin Ash)

The key is to sell the most **exciting** products **out there** says the creative director

Gross signs off the final
look of Ducati's packaging
as well as handling the
wider marketing policies.
(Kevin Ash)

good at moving in and making a company work efficiently as a factory with its own management methods, but you can't just create a brand from scratch with values like those of Ducati.'

What Gross says next underlines the dramatic and innovative approach of the Americans – it's obvious in retrospect and it's easy to agree with it because it is evidently working, but it's the reverse of what the previous management under the Castiglioni brothers were doing and what many others would have done.

'The factory was full of old and inefficient machinery. There was even this ancient, huge thing we used to call Big Bertha, used for machining. So what did we do with our first round of investment? We built a museum!'

The Americans, with the advantage of experience in turning around established brands and with the perspective only available to outsiders, saw that the value of Ducati lay not in the physical condition of the factory or its machinery, but in the brand itself. Indeed, as with the majority of motorcycle companies, a very large proportion of the components which make up each Ducati motorcycle aren't even produced at the factory. Some are obviously outsourced, such as the brakes and wheels from Brembo-Marchesini, the Showa, Öhlins and Paioli suspension and of course the tyres. The plastic bodywork also comes from an outside supplier and the frames too are built elsewhere. A great many engine components are cast, forged or machined before they arrive in Borgo Panigale and pistons are bought complete from a specialist company. This is why there is so much emphasis placed on the museum and why so many people are encouraged to see it – it has been central to TPG's investment both physically and metaphorically.

Gross has no doubts at all: 'The museum is incredibly important, and after that the Motogiro event which we are just reviving. It gives people activities to see and do and involves them.

'The world we then built up around Ducati was centred on the fact that Ducati was a motorcycle company which raced. There was nothing altruistic or self indulgent in that as it's a great way to sell all sorts of apparel and accessories from T-shirts to performance parts. And central to the racing effort is the enormous excitement it generates for the brand and the way it maintains a level of authenticity. The key for Ducati is producing the most exciting product out there.' There's no doubting this – nothing can justify a rider's choice of sporting road bike better than a clearly related racing equivalent winning the World Superbike Championship. Without its race successes over the last decade Ducati road bikes would have nothing like the credibility they enjoy today. In fact, it was only from 2000 that TPG started to pour the bulk of its investment into the design and production side of Ducati, after the brand had been strengthened sufficiently to benefit from that.

But there was plenty more that Gross saw had to be changed. 'The brand had lots of logos, which wasn't satisfactory. We had to make a change anyway because Cagiva had retained the rights to the main one, so we introduced the new logo and used it consistently right across the range and in all our other branded material. We had to do this to appear professional – Ducati could not continue to be just a local European thing, it had to be global like all the other major brands. It's a big business and has to behave like one.'

It's an approach which has worked fabulously well but it has created some conflicts. Design chief Pierre Terblanche had to fight tooth and nail to get the old logo on to the side of the MH900e. He says that in the end he sneaked it on without anyone spotting it until it was too late! Yet how inappropriate the current logo would have looked in its place.

Gross also initiated the Ducati People advertising campaign. It was not quite along the lines of this book as it concentrated on values centred on youth, Italian-ness, real people: 'This was a powerful strategy against the Japanese,' says Gross. 'They build some amazing products, but they're not characterised by heritage or history. Inevitably they have to be dumbed down, homogenic, perfect, in order to appeal to the widest mass market. Ducati is different.

'On the business side we concentrated on selling families of bikes, avoiding the usual approach which focuses on horsepower or financing and so on. This is important, as we've seen the trend for motorcycles to become art and be collectible. Our involvement with the Guggenheim and the Art of the Motorcycle exhibition was a great success.

'But we are aware that you can go too far in this approach – you can get too corporate, but we want to keep the traditional old Ducati enthusiasts. It's especially satisfying when you can put

the old and new ones together and see it working, as at the World Ducati Weekend.'

Gross, careful to give credit where it is due, won't accept any responsibility on his or TPG's behalf for Ducati's track successes though. 'Ducati was already winning long before TPG came into the picture,' he says. 'But what we did was build a world around that.

'The quality of the bikes is now much better, which helps, but Ducati was thinking of dropping its desmodromic valves and using alternatives to the V-twin configuration!' He is genuinely quite horrified at the very idea, understanding that these characteristics are so closely associated with Ducati they've come to be part of the definition of Ducati. It's here that his initial marketing role overlaps the product development with which he is now more heavily involved on a day to day basis.

'The Ducati image side of my job is now done. It has gained its own momentum and it looks after itself, so I don't need to do that any more,' he says.

Just when it looked as if there might be a small break in the relentless torrent of words, Gross expands on the TPG input. 'This is a glorious story for TPG, a real textbook takeover for a venture capital company. So many takeovers can be ugly, painful things, with lots of people being fired, assets being sold and so on. But over the last few years we've hired around 500 people, the company's growing and it's looking so good.

'This is a very special company though. Ones like it are so rare – maybe you'd get the same with a soccer team, a film maker possibly, Ferrari of course, and Harley-Davidson.

'This is one of the great companies of the world.'

David Gross respected the essence of Ducati, keeping that pure while the management was modernised. (Ducati)

There was always an inevitability about Livio Lodi becoming employed at Ducati. His mother and father met in the Bologna suburb of Borgo Panigale where the factory's located, they lived in the area and in 1955 his father became the doctor assigned to the factory. In 1971, at the age of five, Lodi's brother took him to the factory for the first time, and he became a regular visitor as a schoolboy during most of the holidays, such as at Easter and over Christmas. Rather more unlikely were the circumstances in which Lodi eventually began work at Ducati. After leaving school he studied accountancy, passing his degree in 1986, and with this he applied for a job, which was pretty much assured considering his father's connection. Come April 1987 and the factory telephoned, asking him and his twin brother both to report for work.

Which is where the story takes a rather bizarre turn. Lodi explains: 'I turned up in what I thought was appropriate dress, all neat in a suit, and I asked where my office was. They gave me a very odd look and said "what do mean, your office? You're working down there!" They were pointing at the production line!'

Lodi had indeed been taken on as a production line worker, despite applying for an accountancy position, and without even being told beforehand. But what the hell, this was still a job with Ducati, and he took it anyway! 'My brother was given the same job as me, and because he was right handed and I'm left handed, they set us up at one point on the production line with him on one side and me on the other!'

Lodi's first job was fitting fairings to the Paso, something which was not as easy as it should have been. 'They never fitted properly, so we'd been given special mini-cookers for heating water on so that it could be used to soften the plastic to make it easier to bend and get the fairing to fit. In the winter the shop floor used to become very cold, so we used those cookers to make our coffee on instead.'

The production quality in those days was not very good. 'I think every Paso fairing was different to the next one,' says Lodi. 'Some of them used to come with scratches on, too. They should have been sent back of course, but instead I was given the job of trying to put

Livio Lodi is a man with a quest required. He found the Apollo prototype in Japan and brought it home. (Kevin Ash)

Finding the Apollo prototype was
the assistant curator's personal odyssey

them right with touch-up paint. I was a keen modeller so they thought I'd be right for this job! But these were brand new bikes to go in showrooms, and they'd been repaired with touch-up paint! I remember too working on the 851 line when one of the bosses came along and asked what we thought of it. I pointed out where there were some holes which were supposed to line up with parts of the frame, and how they'd vary in position by almost two centimetres! It never got better while I was there...' But it's not just the detail of production which Lodi recalls. 'It's different for the workers who arrive at Ducati today. Now there's a much stronger, more secure feeling. In the 1980s people used to be constantly worried about their future. Now the company has done well, and you get the feeling that it really believes in the power of every worker.'

Lodi's eye-opening stint on the production line lasted for one year, after which he was, finally, drafted into the accountancy department. Here his job involved compiling production data which he then evaluated to establish estimated values for individual departments within Ducati. Ultimately the job was boring, one of the reasons he eventually asked to do something different. Another influence was the death of his mother in 1987, an event which upset him badly and made him wonder about his future.

Yet that intimate knowledge of various Ducati departments was to prove extremely useful later. Lodi had nurtured a passion for history ever since the age of five when an image of First World War German aviator Manfred von Richthofen, the Red Baron, stuck vividly in his head. At the same tender and highly formative age, Lodi was also enormously influenced by Steve McQueen in the racing car film *Le Mans*, propagating his love of racing, its characters and tying it in neatly to his historical leanings.

Motor racing, history, a family in Borgo Panigale, a father who worked at Ducati – how could Lodi not have worked for the company? His fascination for the First World War is just as strong today and he's an expert on the tanks used in the conflict – there's even a German Army helmet from the period in his office. But it's an interest which, in a slightly obtuse way, proved useful rather than diversionary. Lodi's difficulty was that most of the best books on the world

wars are written in English, motivating him to learn the language which he now speaks fluently. As a result, when the Americans took control at the end of 1996, Lodi was one of relatively few people who could communicate with them easily. He had also acquired an encyclopaedic knowledge of Ducati's history, and with the Americans concentrating on Ducati the brand ahead even of Ducati the factory – as David Gross explains in his chapter – Lodi was suddenly an extremely valuable asset.

They'd also seen him throw himself into the organisation of the first World Ducati Weekend in 1998, and he was offered the opportunity to work in the newly set-up Ducati museum, where he is now immersed in a world which could hardly be better matched to his talents and passions, as assistant curator. His job was and still is researching, investigating and collating material, and his eyes light up when he talks about it:

'I found an elderly lady, 83 years old, who used to be the secretary of Adriano Ducati, one of the three brothers who founded the company. She introduced me to many more people who used to work for Ducati in the 1930s, including some who remembered when Il Duce, Mussolini, once visited the factory. I feel that it's absolutely essential to preserve the memories of these people, because it's what gives the factory life today. We've spent a lot of money on the work – recently we reprinted some 700 pictures which have never been published before.'

Lodi is fiercely proud of his most recent mission. 'I remember when I was being shown my job by my mentor, Giuliano Pedretti, the curator – I am so grateful to him for all his help – he

Lodi's knowledge is vast. Ask him about a bike and he'll tell you the day and time the production line started to roll! (Kevin Ash)

showed me this enormous, dusty engine. I hadn't seen it before and didn't know the bike it was from, but the shape was still familiar, even though it was some 30 years old. It was from a bike called the Apollo, a name which stuck in my head as it sounded modern, despite the age.'

The Apollo project was instigated in the early 1960s by the American Ducati importer Berliner, which wanted a machine aimed at the lucrative police market dominated by Harley-Davidson and BMW. The ever prolific Fabio Taglioni produced a 1,257cc 90° V-four with five-speed gearbox, a major departure from the small, single-cylinder machines for which Ducati was better known.

The bike was fascinating for several reasons. Because of its then enormous power output – 80bhp for the police version and a breathtaking 100bhp for a proposed sports alternative (at a time when pace-setting British twins were producing around half that) – it featured a double drive chain to the back wheel, and to keep the engine compact it had a very short stroke relative to its bore size, with dimensions of 84.5mm x 56mm. This bore to stroke ratio is more typical of modern multi-cylinder supersports bikes.

The familiarity which nagged at Lodi came from the cooling fins in addition to the 90° angle between front and rear cylinders. As on the Ducati V-twins which came after the Apollo, those on the front cylinders were aligned parallel to the bore while those on the rear were arranged more conventionally across it.

The Apollo never went into production as it proved just too powerful and heavy for the tyres of the day – the dry weight was around 270kg (600lb). Reducing the power was tried but

Lodi was a prime organiser of the first World Ducati Weekend in 1998, which attracted around 10,000 Ducati fans. (Kevin Ash)

didn't work as the performance became inadequate with so much mass to lug around and the project was dropped. Lodi knew that apart from the engine in the museum, there was still somewhere in the world a complete Apollo prototype in existence, and he made it his personal goal to find that bike.

'At first I had no luck, but then a Japanese journalist I was talking to at the first World Ducati Weekend said he thought there was one in Japan. I asked him if he could find out some more, but didn't hear anything for a long time. Then out of the blue, he sent me a picture of the bike and the address it was at. I contacted Ducati Japan to see if they could persuade the owner to sell it, but he didn't want to. He wasn't even keen on loaning it to us, but we said we would restore it for him and he agreed.'

The bike is important to Lodi for two reasons: it holds a special place in Ducati's history as the link between Ducati's singles and the V-twins which followed. This was the first Ducati 90° V, and the first to feature that distinctive finning, and there's no question Taglioni used other things he learned while designing the Apollo when later working on the V-twins.

It also means a lot to Lodi personally. 'I remember when showing people around the museum how they were always impressed by the first Ducati, the little Cucciolo, and how they never failed to be amazed at the size of the Apollo engine. There seemed to be such a gap in the collection where the complete bike should have been.

'Finding it was like discovering the *Titanic* for me! And finding it in 2001 was significant. This was the year depicted in the film *2001: A Space Odyssey* – finding this bike had been my own personal odyssey.'

Now the bike has arrived, Livio Lodi has hardly relaxed – you're more likely to spot him pounding the corridors of the factory as he chases up information or pictures for the many journalists and researchers who know and admire his fabulously detailed knowledge, or as he goes about his ongoing task of compiling what will surely be the ultimate, definitive Ducati archive.

He deserves a prominent place in it.

There is a handful of key figures in Ducati's history who deserve accreditation as being fundamental to the company's survival, men without whom it's fair to say Ducati would no longer be in business. One of those, undoubtedly, is Gianluigi Mengoli, who today is Ducati's technical director, overseeing everything from the new projects department to everyday production. His job is to guide the younger engineers, to ensure projects follow the intended direction, overcome production line difficulties and to deal with any other problems his vast experience puts him in a position to solve.

Apart from anything else, Mengoli is one of the longest serving of Ducati's staff, having started at the company in 1966, although he doesn't count himself among the many whose life's dream it was to work at the Bologna factory. In fact, he wasn't even interested in motorcycles: 'My real passion was for engines,' he says. 'I used to live in the countryside on a farm, as a small boy. My grandfather had tractors and other sorts of big machinery, and my fascination for engines came from being around them.'

Mengoli's first real job certainly involved machinery, but of a different sort – he started with a linotype and printing company called Simoncini, working with the printing presses. But there was a Ducati connection: both the director and director general of Simoncini were ex-employees of Ducati, and the two companies had a good working relationship. Mengoli often found himself working on design projects for Ducati which had been sub-contracted to Simoncini.

It was here that Mengoli gained his real grounding in engineering design skills, impressing his peers and superiors with his skills, and he also became known at Ducati for his ability. At the same time, during the early 1960s, the introduction of new printing technology was causing problems in the industry, and Simoncini was badly affected. Even though it was a big company with some 250 employees it was forced into liquidation, so the natural step for Mengoli was to move over to work directly for Ducati – he'd proved his talent, knew a lot about how the company worked, and for him it was a chance to indulge his great passion for engines.

From the outset Mengoli was working directly under Fabio Taglioni, a man for whom he has great admiration without being blinded to any faults. 'Taglioni had this fantastic energy,' says

Gianluigi Mengoli worked in secret on the design of the eight-valve desmo twin with Massimo Bordi, it's a favourite. (Kevin Ash)

and techno

A tiny little flame was all that was left
of Ducati, recalls the technical director

Mengoli. 'He was constantly wanting to do new things and to take on new projects – his enthusiasm was enormous. But this wasn't always for the good. He was especially passionate about racing – this came above everything else. But it meant he often didn't really focus on what the customers of the road bikes wanted. I think the design and production of road bikes definitely suffered because of this. Even so, I have always counted myself as very lucky to have worked with this man.'

Taglioni clearly had plenty of respect for Mengoli, as the two worked together right up to the 1980s. From 1978 every single Ducati project was done by Taglioni and Mengoli on a more or less equal basis. Mengoli was in charge of the Pantah project, a bike whose legacy is still with Ducati today as the SS models are all directly descended from it. This was the bike which moved Ducati on from the effective but expensive bevel-driven overhead camshafts to the automotive-style inverted tooth belt (not used by any other motorcycle manufacturer). But this was carried out against a background of increasing disillusionment with Ducati, or at least, with the way the company was being run by its government owners. (Ducati had been state owned since the late 1940s). The

government had decided that Ducati's future lay in producing diesel engines rather than motorcycles, and the policy was pursued to the point where the 20 people involved in motorcycle production in 1973 had been whittled down to just two by 1980.

Mengoli remembers these as dark times: 'The atmosphere was not good at the end of the 1970s, and it was getting worse and worse into the '80s. A lot of people left the company and the only ones remaining were those who had a real passion for what they were doing. There was no other reason to stay as the place was being run down.' Mengoli proved his

Mengoli oversees the whole of Ducati's new model design, where his talent engenders great respect. (Kevin Ash)

loyalty to the Ducati cause at this point by doing more than just staying – he and Franco Farnè continued to keep Ducati's race programme going as best they could, even though it meant paying for a lot of the costs themselves!

'There was much goodwill towards Ducati then and many people realised the difficulties we were going through. A lot of other motorcycle factories, tyre companies and so on used to help us out – even our competitors – making parts for us, doing us special favours, giving us spares and equipment. I couldn't tell you even now who some of them were because they really shouldn't have been doing it, but we were very grateful of course.' This is really quite astonishing, that some of the very companies Ducati was trying to beat on the race tracks were quietly helping Mengoli and Farnè with their race effort. It gives some idea of how strong the value is of motorcycle sport to a company which attracts such a passionate, dedicated following. It also shows what many have always suspected, that even those who work for rival companies have a sneaking respect for what Ducati has been able to achieve with its relatively tiny budgets and minimum of staff, first against the might of the big European companies, and then the huge resources and facilities of the Japanese.

But despite all this dedication and goodwill, with Ducati's bosses failing to understand what they had in their charge and with bike production all but fizzling out, for Mengoli the future was very bleak: 'A tiny little flame was all that was left, that was all. We nurtured it as best we could, but it was only a matter of time before it was snuffed out completely.'

Then, right as Ducati teetered on the very edge of its existence, with production down to less than 3,000 bikes a year, you could almost hear the blast of bugles as the cavalry charged to the rescue in the form of the Castiglioni brothers, Claudio and Gianfranco. It was not quite the straightforward takeover that many people imagine as the Castiglionis' Cagiva company originally asked only for a supply of Ducati engines which were to power Cagiva motorcycles, the plan being to phase out production of Ducati-badged machines altogether.

But even though the engines were the same, Cagiva as a new and unknown company simply could not generate the fervent following of Ducati, so in 1985 the Castiglionis bought Ducati complete, injecting desperately needed funds and a great new hope with them.

They recognised immediately that Mengoli's Pantah was the machine they should concentrate on, as the old bevel drive engines could no longer be produced profitably. But while his project was already playing its part in reviving the famous factory, Mengoli himself had become involved in another, even more influential project. A new, young engineer called Massimo Bordi had joined Ducati with ideas about producing an eight-valve version of the V-twin engine, in order to keep pace with modern thinking. But it wasn't well received by everyone, according to Mengoli: 'Taglioni was getting old. He was less decisive than he had been in the past and his health wasn't so good. And he simply didn't want an eight-valve engine – he was against the idea.'

But Bordi and Mengoli knew this was the way forward, so they designed the new engine, in secret at home! At the same time, the two engineers designed a new set of crankcases for the Pantah engine so its capacity could be increased to 900cc from the original's 500cc – it had already been taken out to 750cc, but couldn't be extended beyond this without major changes. They also had in mind the possibility of using these cases for the liquid-cooled, eight-valve engine they were planning, so the concentration on the Pantah proved fortuitous.

Even aside from having to work absurdly long hours in his spare time, Mengoli was faced with the inevitable additional difficulties a new engine design will always throw up. At one stage he decided he needed some outside help with the cylinder head design, so he contacted the British race engine manufacturer and consultancy Cosworth, but was turned away. 'Cosworth didn't want to know about anything to do with desmo valves! They wouldn't touch our design.

Mengoli stuck with Ducati in its darkest hour, playing a pivotal role in bringing the company out into the light once again. (Ducati)

'After this it was just my pride which kept me going. I was determined to finish this engine, forcing myself to find a solution. I think when you have your darkest moments, when you're really backed into a corner, that's when your very best ideas come out.'

The engine Mengoli is talking about – incorporating his very best ideas – has proved to be arguably the most successful motor in the history of motorcycle racing. From its original 748cc capacity it grew to 851cc, 888cc and then to the still current 916cc as the motive source for one of the great motorcycles of the last century, gaining even more cc's to become the 996 and 998, in each incarnation the capacity giving the bike its name.

The brilliance of the design is even more astonishing when you discover not just the circumstances in which it was conceived and created, but the timetable Mengoli and Bordi were up against. They started the project, from scratch, in September 1985; by March 1986 most of the engine was finished, and by 30 April the most difficult part of the project, the desmodromic, four-valve cylinder heads – greatly influenced by contemporary thinking in Formula One car engine design – had been completed. Another month and the motor, with its new-to-Ducati fuel injection system, was producing 93bhp on the test bench.

In August 1986, the bike entered the Bol d'Or, a gruelling 24-hour endurance race, the three-rider team comprising Marco Lucchinelli, Juan Garriga and Virginio Ferrari. The bike immediately proved its speed, matching the four-cylinder machines in this respect and was in seventh place out of some 40 starters when a failed conrod bolt put it out of action – unsurprising in a brand new engine practically thrown together in a matter of months. But at the same time, the old Taglioni

Mengoli gives similar attention to race and road bike components, so vital is the track/street relationship. (Kevin Ash)

school of engines was doing even better, the 860cc version of the Pantah motor producing a reliable 95bhp, and Mengoli's and Bordi's motor came close to being dropped. It's quite probable Ducati would by now be out of business if this decision had been made.

Instead the project continued, Mengoli and Bordi levelling the odds by increasing the capacity of their engine to 851cc, which is when its huge advantage became clear – the power rocketed to 115bhp, even though the Pantah motor was benefiting from years of development and the eight-valve engine was only just starting its life. The old Pantah design was completely eclipsed, opening up a new and even more successful era for Ducati while vindicating the dogged determination and sheer hard work of Mengoli and Bordi.

Mengoli, more perhaps than Taglioni, sees the relationship between race bikes and the road machines as very important for Ducati. 'The race bikes and production bikes are completely integrated. The magic of Ducati comes from one feeding off the other – you must have both together.' He sees the road bikes' development accelerated by the race programme, which is why Ducati races in classes where the competition machines are based on road bikes, feeding the excitement of road riders, who see machines similar to their own battling it out on the race tracks – and very often, winning.

Even after all his years at Ducati, Mengoli still gets very excited about this. 'At the World Superbike round at Monza the people around me tried to calm me down. They said if I carried on like I was they'd have to take me to the medical tent!

'But there is so much of our people in our products, you can't help feeling that way. Whenever I take anybody new on, the first thing I check is to see if they have that passion. It's very important as this goes into the products, and it's what makes Ducati special.'

Mengoli now is as contented as he's ever been, thoroughly enjoying his time at Ducati. 'It's enormously stimulating working on the race bikes, and the new superbike project.

'But I love to see so many young faces around, it really means a lot to me to have this new lifeblood in the factory. They could almost be my children!'

Children with an astonishing legacy in their hands, courtesy Luigi Mengoli.

Federico Minoli, in many envious eyes, surely has the ultimate toy – he is the big boss in charge of the Ducati factory, the president of the sexiest motorcycle company in the world, the man with the final say on new models, who rides for the race team, how many bikes should be produced, how the company should be run. It's not a toy though, and he doesn't play at being in control. This is for real, and the buck stops right on the desk in front of him.

Minoli, who speaks in near-flawless American English, was put into place with overall charge of the Ducati Group of companies by the Texas Pacific Group when it bought Ducati in 1996, a role he has carried out successfully with other companies taken over by the American venture capital group. Minoli's tasks include presenting a public face for Ducati, acting as point of contact at the highest level, and after that to deal with and make the final decision on all sorts of issues and problems. But this is certainly not done on the hoof: 'A plan for Ducati was put into place when TPG took control in 1996 as part of the new shareholder structure, with TPG then set up as the majority shareholder. That strategy continues to be valid today and will be valid for the forseeable future. My job is to ensure that Ducati management adheres to that strategy.'

The takeover was far from straightforward – in fact Minoli says it was the most difficult one that TPG has ever been involved in. 'The negotiations were extremely difficult, partly because of cultural differences between the Italians and Americans and partly because we were buying a family-owned company with much personal involvement.' He adds diplomatically: 'The accounting was very sparse, too...' In all, it took a year and a half to acquire Ducati from previous owners, the Castiglioni brothers, who had incorporated it into their Cagiva Group of motorcycle companies, and Minoli wouldn't have been surprised if it hadn't happened at all. 'There was one day we call Black Friday. One international lawyer was called back from his holiday in Katmandhu, while TPG director Abel Halpern had to break into his honeymoon so that the papers could be signed. We had on hold six million dollars in expenses accrued to get the deal this far, and... the Castiglionis didn't turn up! At that point we felt like simply jumping on a plane to Brazil or somewhere and disappearing off the face of the earth. It was very, very stressful!'

The deal was concluded eventually, a tie-up which time has proved turned the company right

The sharp but amiable Ducati president Federico Minoli. He had more stress buying the company than running it. (Kevin Ash)

The president who felt TPG had
acquired something very precious

around, but things didn't get any easier in the first year or so in which TPG, via Minoli, was in control. 'It was not easy to clean up the company in the beginning. We obliterated the commercial department apart from two staff (including Piero Guidi, now the boss of Ducati UK), losing 20 people in a week. This meant we had no sales staff, nobody to look after that side of the business.'

These sometimes sweeping changes extended beyond the factory itself as Minoli saw the dealer network and importer systems needed to be radically overhauled, too. Around 90 per cent of the various importers around the world were changed, mostly being brought under the direct control of the factory, while the 200 Ducati dealers in Italy were slashed to just 55, a thinning out of the network which was reflected in many other countries. It had to be done, but Minoli didn't find it especially easy: 'All of these people and companies had such close and real attachments to Ducati and to the Castiglioni family – this was a really painful experience to have to go through.'

The question begs: why bother? Why the tortuous, protracted and anguished negotiations, the pain of upsetting and losing so many close friends of the factory? 'In the end, of course it was because we saw the possibility of making money. It doesn't matter how you dress that up, that's the bottom line,' says Minoli, with disarming honesty. 'You have to believe you're going to make money or what are you doing here?' But it was Minoli who wrote the due diligence report on Ducati for TPG, the document which describes not just what a company's position is at the time, but its potential, how the markets it operates in are behaving and so on. And Minoli saw something very special indeed: 'My conclusion was that we were trying to buy something very precious, of which there are very few examples anywhere in the world. These are brands or products that mean something extra to a niche of very passionate people.'

The physical state of the Ducati factory, the way its distribution networks were organised and so on didn't even matter a great deal to Minoli and TPG. As far as they were concerned, Ducati was not even a real company, more a sort of family concern with what he describes as '...a primitive distribution network, primitive systems, primitive plant. But these are all elements which can be fixed by good management within two or three years. It takes far more time and much, much more investment to build a brand from scratch, and even with good management you can't guarantee to do that. So it was very clear to us we were buying into a major brand, not some plant or distribution network, and that was much more valuable.' This is typical of the way TPG operates, searching the world for old, prestigious brand names – they might be disastrous as companies, but TPG's skill is in fixing companies, making them run properly and efficiently, leaving it with a well-run brand name which has a massively increased value as a consequence.

So the money-making ethic stems from choosing a brand, not buildings or machinery, and in Ducati TPG saw a brand so powerful, it was prepared to endure those eighteen months of its worst ever negotiations. Minoli's actions underline this approach. 'My priorities when I came in were evident. Rather than fix the roof – and I mean that literally, it was leaking badly! – I built a museum. This was because to us the heritage and the brand and the history are more important than the building itself.'

Minoli's calculated evaluation of Ducati as a brand name capable of generating profits hides how he's been caught up in the Ducati phenomenon as much as anyone else. 'Being boss of Ducati is a very cool job!' he says, laughing. 'In 1998, when it was clear the factory really was turning around, that's when it all started to become fun. It's now the most enjoyable job I've ever had in all my managerial experience. The difference here is the bond which links you to everyone else at Ducati, and it's not just the workers but our customers too. See that letter there, on the wall?' He points to one of several pinned to a board opposite his desk. 'Whenever I see a Ducati parked up in my travels around the world in some obscure location, I leave my business card and a note saying something like, 'what are you doing here, how do you like the bike', stuff like that. At least 50 per cent of people reply with an answer. That letter came after I saw a Monster in a tiny town in Wyoming, population of 72, parked up outside the Cowboy Saloon. I was with my wife and we thought we'd go in to say hello to the owner. He turned out to be a gay Boeing engineer...'

The Boeing engineer later wrote to Minoli to express his appreciation at meeting him, and it was this which gave Minoli the idea for his Ducati People advertising campaign and a book produced by the factory on same lines. He saw how Ducati was capable of bringing together some very different people from all over the world, which is why he's now working on another project. 'I want

For his 50th birthday
Minoli received a Monster
fuel tank painted with
himself and other Ducati
images. (Kevin Ash)

to get 10,000 pictures sent to us through our website from Ducati riders everywhere, so we can create a huge mural from all of them at the entrance to the factory. We'll do something like give a dollar or so to the Riders For Health charity for each picture.' This idea gives a clue as to what Minoli believes is the essence of Ducati's appeal. 'When you boil it right down, it's all about being in a tribe, being different to the masses, being seen not to have made the obvious choice, but a qualified decision. It happens with us and it happens with Harley-Davidson. Our customers are the same in fact – 60 per cent of Ducatisti in the US also own a Harley.'

This makes a lot of sense as the two types of bike, in being so different dynamically, complement each other in the type of riding they can offer. As Minoli says, the Harley is fine for cruising at 55mph down some endlessly long highway in Wyoming, while the Ducati is the tool for dispatching a twisting, demanding canyon road. 'And with both of these bikes you don't get confused with all the Japanese bike owners. You also want to own a piece of art, a piece of something you can really relate to. Something you can put in your living room!'

So Minoli has become a Ducatisti himself, and more surprisingly, in its own corporate way, so has TPG. The venture capital group has no immediate plans to leave Ducati and still retains a 33 per cent share (which as Minoli points out, at $120 million is practically a rounding-off error for this fabulously wealthy company). 'I think they're as caught up in the passion as everyone else,' he says. 'There's no real reason for them to stay, so it's more affection which is keeping them here.'

There is certainly no real business sense in TPG staying as Ducati has lived up to all its expectations. If TPG were to pull out in 2001, it would make a financial return of around six times its original investment.

Those bruising negotiations, the broken holiday and honeymoon, were all worth it from a business sense then, but how does Minoli feel about the Castiglionis for making life so difficult? The answer is surprising: 'I have a great deal of respect for the Castiglioni brothers. They were very tough negotiators but I survived that as a friend of both Claudio and Giancarlo.'

Minoli sees them, as do many others at the factory, as the saviours of Ducati back in 1985. Without them he wouldn't be boss now. And he just wouldn't be as cool.

The president of Ducati, Federico Minoli, was talking to 26-year-old Marco Montemaggi at a World Superbike round at Misano, near Rimini. They knew each other reasonably well, and Montemaggi at the time was busy building the foundations for a career as a journalist, having acquired a masters degree in marketing and business studies. Montemaggi still looks back with incredulity at what happened next: 'First Minoli asked me if I wanted to work for Ducati. I said no, I wanted to be a journalist. He just ignored that and said, "What I want you to do is a museum. You have six months to complete it, not a lot of money and maybe three or four people to help. And you have five seconds to give me an answer." I hadn't even considered the idea of working for Ducati, let alone doing something like a museum. Of course, I knew a little about Ducati – I owned a Honda at the time so I knew something about motorcycles – but not the history in such great detail that I thought I was qualified to do a Ducati museum! "You now have two seconds" Minoli said to me. So I accepted!'

This wasn't entirely whimsical on the part of Minoli. The Ducati boss was aware that Montemaggi had been involved in the preparations for a Ferrari museum, albeit in a minor way, which was originally going to be sited in San Marino (although it was later decided to base it in Maranello). In Italy there are no courses or specific training for museum curators, so this was as good a grounding as anyone was likely to have, while Montemaggi's journalist training seemed likely to prove useful in tracking down obscure and unique motorcycles.

In many ways too it was still the sort of thing from which Montemaggi knew he'd gain a lot of satisfaction – something solid and tangible which he could point at and say he'd created, as he could do with a piece of writing. Once decided, Montemaggi immersed himself in his mission – with no family ties or other interferences he quickly found himself working seven days a week. 'At weekends I spent most of the time chasing the bikes we wanted to put in the museum, and during the week I spent a lot of time with the architects.'

Two architects were involved, one from Bologna and the other from Florence, whose task was to produce a design for a museum which fitted within the space allocated for it inside the main factory building. It was a space many would say was entirely appropriate – previously the room

In setting up the stunning Ducati museum Marco Montemaggi focused on the emotions as much as the machines. (Kevin Ash)

The museum is almost a **religious**
experience thanks to this curator's zeal

had been used as the company's chapel! Judging by the reaction of people entering it today, the room is still a religious experience for many. Even aside from the fabulous machinery it encloses, the museum itself is quite breathtaking. It comprises a large, circular room with motorcycles lined up around the outside wall, all standing on a translucent floor which provides some stunning lighting effects. Above the bikes are huge pictures of great events, machines and riders from Ducati's past which curve inwards over the bikes so they're easily seen even from up close.

In the centre of the room is an enclosed auditorium, shaped like a crash helmet with seats inside aligned to face outwards through the 'visor' opening, in front of which speakers can give talks from a podium. The bikes are arranged in chronological order around the room, starting with the first, 1946 Cucciolo, and finishing with a current superbike race machine. Leading off the main room are six smaller ones, each with a particularly special machine or story to tell. It's all beautifully executed and a great tribute to Montemaggi and the effort he's put into it. Unsurprisingly, it didn't come easily: 'When we studied the Ducati story, we found many books on certain events in the history, such as Hailwood's TT win, Paul Smart or the Marianna, but nothing with a full, integrated history. So we had to put this together ourselves, and we had plenty of help from all sorts of people. We even pieced together all of Ducati's victories, which came to more than 3,000!

'Originally we divided the story into ten main families, representing the technical angle, the racing, the people and so on, and we were going to have one room dedicated to each. In the end we reduced this to six rooms because of the space we had, but it's interesting that now a lot of

Montemaggi's magic captured the moods and feelings which drive Ducati and preserved the Ducati spirit. (Kevin Ash)

recent books have been using our classification of these ten families,' which all came from this 26-year-old man who did not then know much about Ducati! Montemaggi wanted this to be a memorable museum, rather than just a room full of motorcycles. So there had to be an appeal to the emotions, which is why the huge pictures line the walls, making a big impact on people as soon as they come through the entrance. 'But we also needed the traditional museum approach,' he says. 'It's important too to have the documentation, the videos, the information, so people feel they know more about Ducati when they walk out than when they came in. If we reach them with this as well as the emotion, then it has been a success.'

The central crash helmet auditorium brings even more life to the museum as it turns it into a room which is constantly being used – a great idea, but it still left Montemaggi with the problem of finding bikes to put in the museum! He started off with six or seven bikes which were either at the factory or which belonged to people very close to it, but many more than these were needed. And at first it was very difficult: 'When I started, no-one was interested, partly because they didn't know who I was and also of course because I was asking for racing bikes which are very special to people. But as I started moving around and being seen in the classic bike market in various countries, things started to get easier.

'One of the first bikes I got was Paul Smart's – he gave it to me personally, and I have to thank him for that because it was very important to the museum.' But it was important for another reason – the arrival of Smart's bike gave the museum credibility and it allowed Montemaggi to turn the tables when he was trying to prise motorcycles out of people. 'At first people would say no, this is my bike, you're just a man I don't know from another country. So I would point out what machines we already had and they would say: "Ah! If so-and-so's bike is in the museum, then I want my bike to be in there too…"' Montemaggi is very happy with the museum now, but although his title is still chief curator he's moving on to other things, such as the running of the World Ducati Weekends, the new Motogiro and other events which are planned. He can do so in the knowledge that his creation is central to the new strategy for Ducati, part of the plan to turn the company around and into a brand whose business is as strong as its passion.

M ost Ducati fans can cite two epochal race wins by the Bologna bikes during the 1970s, those of Paul Smart and Mike Hailwood. But American fans and the real cognoscenti elsewhere will always relate a third example, the seemingly unlikely victory of privateer Cook Neilson at the 1977 Daytona Superbike race.

Neilson, at the time, was editor of the big circulation motorcycle magazine *Cycle*, but he was also managing to fit in a respectable race career. Just about... 'We were young enough then to run the magazine during the day, then do everything that had to be done on the bikes in the evenings and other times. You'd often find us asleep in the workshop!'

With his position on the magazine and all the publicity he could accrue, you might think he could have chosen almost any make of bike to race, and as Ducati was almost unknown in the USA in this period his choice of 750SS needs explaining: 'It didn't make sense at the time to have a magazine project involving a Japanese bike as we had to be seen to be impartial. If we'd had one make the others would only have complained about the excessive coverage. But Ducati was obscure and out of the mainstream.'

The choice of Italian bike wasn't purely political, though: 'I didn't know a lot about bikes when we went for the Ducati, but I did know this one was special. I'd grown up with Harleys so I was used to V-twins, and there was this Ducati V-twin with all its noise and power, and it didn't vibrate. It was so little too, so I was always inclined towards it. I liked the Ducati concept of having less power but compensating with very light weight with good handling and brakes. It seemed a natural for racing.

'Then the handling was very slow and predictable which made the bike good for Daytona – this was the race I was always aiming to win, so this was the bike to do it on.'

As well as this, Neilson was racing the bike, which became known as the California Hot Rod, with fellow journalist Phil Schilling, who had been a Ducati fan for many years already, so ultimately it was an obvious choice, not an odd one.

Being such an unusual bike also made for a cracking good series of features in the magazine, which Neilson ran as they prepared and raced it. As far as the readers were

Most magazine project bikes end up unfinished in a shed. Cook Neilson (left) rode his to victory at Daytona. (Phillip Tooth)

This bike became 'the people's favourite'
says racer-cum-magazine editor

concerned the California Hot Rod was the underdog, up against the might of the Japanese four-cylinder machines and established, factory-supported BMW twins, and with only a magazine editor aboard, albeit a fast one.

But Cook Neilson knew better: 'The bike had become almost the "people's favourite" – lots of them knew about it because of our magazine articles, but it was still this strange bike competing at the very highest level which they thought had little real hope of success. But I always thought we had a good chance of winning that race. All our preparation for the previous two years was aimed at winning that one race on that one day – even our two races at Daytona in 1975 and 1976 were really in preparation for 1977.'

For the first outing at Daytona the bike ran in the 750cc class, which almost unnoticed it won. The following year Neilson and Schilling increased the engine capacity to 883cc so it could have a chance of winning outright, and as far as Neilson is concerned the bike was already superior to the opposition: 'In the '76 race the Ducati was the best bike there – it was me who wasn't good enough! We came third, beaten by two works BMWs.'

He had a solution though: 'What we were determined to do was make up for that with the work we had put into the bike, and we did a lot! Every piece of the California Hot Rod was massaged one way or another. A lot of that was just maintenance, but some of it was more serious tuning work. A lot of people were involved with it and we won a lot of local races, but always with that '77 Daytona event in mind.' Neilson and Schilling's confidence grew in the days leading up to the race, despite the public perception of their minimal

The race went remarkably smoothly – Neilson built up such a big lead he could slow down towards the end. (Phillip Tooth)

chance of success. 'We felt that we would win as long as we didn't screw up. During the practice week we knew exactly what the opposition was doing, their lap times and their speed trap figures, and we knew we could beat them. Some of the other bikes were four or five mph quicker than we were through the speed trap, but our bike handled beautifully, it braked well and we knew we could beat them. Even if I had something in reserve I thought I could still do it!'

And that's exactly how it went – Neilson has little to report on the race itself apart from a minor tangle with a Yoshimura in the very early stages before he pulled out a comfortable lead. 'We won by 26, 28 seconds or so, and I even throttled back with two laps to go to make sure we'd finish. I could see how far ahead I was on the big screens they had at Daytona – you have a lot of time there to look around – and when I looked over my shoulder the next bike was a long way behind. The race was over almost before I realised it was happening. When I pulled in I said, "Phil, that was easy!" And it really was.

'It wasn't because I was so great as a rider, either. I'd started too late to make the top levels – there were younger guys than me at Daytona with more years of racing experience, so this was all about the bike.'

Neilson's underselling himself a touch here – maybe he wasn't at the level of the factory riders, but you don't win at Daytona on any bike by being second rate. The bike might have been the exceptional half of the partnership, but still Neilson was very, very fast.

The win had quite an effect on Neilson: 'It was like we'd done the job. We'd focused on that race, intending to win it, and that's just what we did. I thought about stopping right there. I did one race at the end of the year and called it a day. And happily so – the rules were changing in the wrong direction for us to have the advantages we did – for example, in '77 we were able to have a better exhaust than most of the competition, which a lot of work went into.'

Neilson remembers that particularly fondly: 'That exhaust was great, the most salient part of the bike – it sounded like Jack the Bear! I rode a works Ducati racer in the mid-1990s and it sounded so quiet in comparison!' The effect of the win on the race-going public was just as big – this was Ducati's dramatic arrival across the Atlantic, the race which thrust its name into the mainstream and in that one win, endowed its badge with instant respect. It had the big advantage of course of serious coverage in a major magazine, but the bike still had to cross the line first at Daytona.

Neilson is quite clear about what the Ducati's advantages were: 'We looked at the whole science of racing in terms of linear distance, imagining a line around a track with a bike going around – how much force can you apply to every part of that line? You break it down into cornering, braking, engine power, and if you can apply more force than anyone else along that whole line, then you win.

'The Ducati was complete, or nearly so, as a package. It lacked some horsepower compared with the Japanese bikes but could still apply more force to that line because of its handling and braking. It only lacked in lower gear acceleration, and we originally had slight cornering problems as it had to lean more because of that long wheelbase. So we made it narrower and higher, and this was no longer an issue.

'The one concern I had late on was whether we could go the full distance with the fuel we had. I'd just assumed it would, but when I looked in the tank afterwards I thought, wow, we only just made it! The bike was doing around 14mpg, where a stock one would do about 45–50mpg, which says how much gas it was flowing. But it was burning efficiently – there was a nice tan ring at the end of the exhaust. I was really surprised at that.'

Neilson's time with the California Hot Rod has left its inevitable impression: 'Ducati is very special to me. I always root for them like mad!

'Harley-Davidson achieved salvation through the vision of Willie G. Davidson who recognised the bikes didn't really matter that much, it was the lifestyle which counted. The same thing seems to be swirling around Ducati, except with them the bikes are really good too. I saw Ben Bostrom get his double win at Laguna Seca in the Superbike race, ahead of the V-twin Hondas. It's not just that the Ducatis are V-twins, it's that they're good V-twins!'

The bevel drive V-twin, named the California Hot Rod, opened American eyes to the existence of Ducati. (Phillip Tooth)

Suzi Perry is the familiar – and much fancied – face of World Superbike race coverage on BBC television, a position she achieved after establishing her credentials as a commentator with Sky TV covering Superbikes, grands prix and speedway, carrying off a breathless, fast-paced and chatty style as she sweeps through pit garages and across packed starting grids with enormous professionalism and informed intelligence.

Looking so good helps too, no question, but it's Suzi's clear enthusiasm for the subject which is infectious, drawing viewers into World Superbikes to the point where they feel involved in a drama rather than being mere observers of racing on a track, aware of the characters as much as the technical details of the motorcycles and the finishing positions. 'I always felt this side of things was missing,' she says. 'Race commentary would give plenty of technical information about the bikes, what tyres riders were using and so on, but very little about the men themselves, what they were feeling, what was motivating them. If there's any one thing I've added to commentary, it's bringing out the characters in the sport. It helps me in the job too, knowing better when I can speak to some people and not others, choosing the right times to ask them difficult questions or to leave them alone.' This is why the teams respect her – an essential asset for her to operate effectively – and this is why she's able to dive beneath a closing pit garage door as the rest of the world is shut out in those intense periods when PR has to take second place to the prime objective, winning a race.

Her position so close to the gritty operating details of the teams gives her a unique insight into the mix of rivalries, intense competition, joy, deep depression and the insane pace of the pit lane, both within and between the teams. She is able to observe first hand exactly how they operate when the pressure is really on, when they're no longer concerned about the public face they're presenting and are simply doing everything in their power to get their rider and motorcycle across the finish line ahead of their rivals.

Despite her need to maintain an element of impartiality, Suzi is in no doubt there is one team which stands out for its sheer passion: 'Every time I walk into the Ducati pit garage it's so alive! Some of that is definitely due to the team manager Davide Tardozzi, but there's a very special

Suzi Perry interviews Briton Neil Hodgson. Her mission is to bring the personalities into racing. (GeeBee Photographic)

The WSB reporter who loves this
Italian soap-opera – it's so alive!

energy in there.' This can be very helpful when Suzi's trying to get a hot interview, but it doesn't always work in her favour: 'Depending on how things are going on the track, it's either really friendly or they can come over rather distant. There doesn't seem to be a middle ground, and you don't get this in any of the other pit garages. Just Ducati.

'There is a sort of dark side, which I suppose is very Italian too. I know how all the other teams are structured, but I'm still cloudy about the way the Ducati team is managed, and it can also be a bit resentful at times, which I find saddening.

'I remember interviewing Tardozzi for *Superbike* magazine about the time Frankie Chili was given the boot by Ducati after his clash with Fogarty when this side of the team really came across. They were also sorry they'd lost Troy Corser, but the atmosphere improved a lot when everything seemed to come back together with the arrival of Troy Bayliss.'

Suzi says you get everything in the Ducati team, good as well as bad: 'The Ducati garage encompasses all of life, right to extremes. I remember at Donington when all the grid was lined up and we couldn't find Troy Bayliss. We wondered where on earth he was, he was just missing, it was amazing! Then we found him still in the pit lane, and there was Tardozzi, on his knees beside him, begging him to use another rear tyre. This is so Ducati, it's like a little soap opera going on. An Italian one!' Oh yes, and at the end of that episode, Tardozzi was proved right. Next week, Bayliss gets his own back...

The passion dominates Ducati and presents a huge contrast to the way the Japanese teams operate. 'Honda has been very successful, and it does this by being methodical and working

Perry on The Edge, a riding skills course she helped promote – nothing to do with Ducati, but guess what bike she's on. (MCIA)

smoothly and consistently,' says Suzi. 'Ducati can look quite haphazard in comparison, and you often see disharmony before suddenly everything comes together and works brilliantly.

'I suppose it's like really passionate sex after a raging argument! You need the clashes to make the highs even better.

'But when Ducati is down it runs so deep. The team feels like it has a hold on the World Superbike Championship, as if this is its right, and it shouldn't be taken away. They were absolutely in pieces, inconsolable, when Honda won the title in 2000.'

The same, passionate feelings are found in many of Ducati's riders, including the man most closely associated with the Bologna factory, Carl Fogarty, and Suzi herself has been deeply affected by them. Two occasions stand out for her. Fogarty had broken his arm badly in Australia early in the season and no-one was sure at that stage whether he'd return to racing again, and Suzi had interviewed him at the World Ducati Weekend. 'I remember everyone at the time was wondering what would happen, if he'd come back, and when I introduced him it suddenly got very difficult. I had a real lump in my throat as I wondered if this would be the last time I would introduce him as World Champion, and when I was doing this, his wife Michaela was sobbing!

'Then at Brands Hatch later in the year, he had just come back in from a demonstration ride in front of 100,000 fans all cheering and some of them even crying, the emotion was palpable, unbelievable. And he told me he was looking for some reason to motivate him to come back, something to get his enthusiasm up to go racing, and I thought, if that ride in front of those fans hadn't been reason enough, then nothing would get him to come back. He'd made no announcement then, and I think he still didn't really know himself, but deep down, I knew Carl Fogarty would retire.'

In the face of all the emotion, not just on this occasion but in the Ducati pit at every Superbike round throughout the season, perhaps it's inevitable that Suzi harbours some special feelings towards Ducati. But there's more to it than that. As a beautiful woman making a high profile impact in a testosterone-drenched, male-dominated world, Suzi is in constant demand for her image to be spread across the covers of lifestyle magazines as well as the specialist motorcycle

After years on opposite sides of the camera, Perry has been joined by Carl Fogarty in the TV team. (GeeBee Photographic)

press. In many of the photographs she's pictured with a motorcycle, but despite the presence of half a dozen or more manufacturers in World Superbike racing, there's only one make she's seen on: 'In every photo I'm seen in with a bike, it's always a Ducati!

'The first motorcycle I had which was just mine was a Ducati Monster 750 – I've still got it – so of course I'd often have my picture taken on that. That was great because I really love that bike, it's like my baby. But even when another bike is brought in for a photo shoot, it'll only be another Ducati, usually a 748 or 996. They're seen as the most stylish and the sexiest bikes by people who are outside motorcycling, and when they want something that looks good to them, they'll go for a Ducati too. But there's another thing about Ducatis I appreciate.

As a woman you often find you attract attention when you arrive on a motorcycle' (as Suzi Perry you attract rather more attention than most women, we suspect) '...and this can get to be a bit of a nuisance. But it's noticeable that when you get off a Ducati, people want to come up and talk about the bike, where with other bikes they seem more interested in watching you shaking your hair out of the helmet!'

Suzi is very aware how the feelings for Ducati extend beyond the racing world to the road bikes, something which was underlined for her at the World Ducati Weekend, the bi-annual event organised by the factory at the Misano race track for Ducati fans to gather and immerse themselves in all things Ducati, and where some 10,000 Ducatis arrive from all around the world. 'I was asked to compere the stage events at the WDW – they knew I had a Monster and that I was a bit of a Ducati fan and asked if I'd like to do it. I thought it was quite an honour at first, and then when I saw how unbelievably huge the event was I was amazed. It looked sensational.'

It also gave Suzi a chance to meet up with an old friend. 'Paul Smart was there, which was great. The very first TV interview I did for Sky was with Paul, and we've had a really good relationship ever since.' This is the final hook perhaps, a big moment in Suzi's own professional past linked to the man responsible for one of the most important events in Ducati's history. Look for the extra sparkle in Suzi's eyes when she's probing one of the Ducati team for some behind-the-scenes information in the frantic, haphazard, emotional Italian pit. This is a place she feels really at home.

When Kristin Schelter started work at Ducati in 1997 the factors working against her were beyond daunting: they were terrifying. In an environment dominated by older Italian men with many years accumulated experience, not just in the motorcycle industry generally but specifically at Ducati itself, here was a young, 27-year-old American female with a background in the fashion industry, charged with the mission of establishing a whole new set of systems and working practices which were completely alien to the way the company had operated to date. Add to this the fact she had been put in position by the Texas Pacific Group, which at the time was regarded with considerable suspicion as a venture capital company who many thought might simply be aiming to strip Ducati of its assets in order to make a quick profit before running away, and it's a wonder she even considered moving to Bologna.

Kristin was originally a journalist covering the luxury goods and fashion industries, which had already brought her into a great deal of contact with Italy as the home of style and innovation. Then, like many journalists, she crossed over into public relations, working first for the Rome-based Bulgari jewellery company before moving to the offices of a major public relations and marketing firm in Milan. It was there that she received a phone call from Abel Halpern of TPG, who knew her from a previous TPG project in the fashion industry – she'd also stuck in his mind because the two had been at the same school together in Philadelphia! 'I wouldn't say we were friends as such at school,' she says. 'He was two years older than me and I didn't really come into contact with him, but Abe was one of those extrovert characters you always remember from schooldays. And he used to act in the theatre with my older sister!

'He thought I was still a journalist and called to see if I knew of any good PR companies in Italy who would be able to deal with the TPG takeover of Ducati, to publicise it and look after the press, as Ducati had no international press office at the time. As it happened, I was already in one! Of course, my boss's eyes lit up when I told him. He was Italian, he was a motorcyclist and he knew all about Ducati, but there I was, at this totally junior level, just arrived and I brought in this potentially huge client. We won the business and I was put on the account.' Kristin laughs, a habit she regularly interrupts her conversation with: 'I was given a bonus of a free trip to Israel! It was

Kristin Schelter's previous bike experience was riding this Yamaha on holiday. Now she has a Monster M750. (Kristin Schelter)

It was no **vacation** setting up a **modern** communication system at Ducati

There aren't many roles
Kristin hasn't filled at
Ducati but she displayed
a special talent as a
brochure model. (Ducati)

ludicrous, if I'd known then what I'd done I'd have asked for a lot more!'

Halpern suggested Kristin should work full time for Ducati, and knowing she was keen to leave Italy, said she could work from New York, although she'd have to go to the factory at first for three months. 'That three months became three years! Luckily, it was a great three years. Abe was a great salesman. I agreed to move to Bologna without even seeing the factory or really knowing what I was letting myself in for. But the day I arrived I had tears in my eyes – I'd just split up with my boyfriend and I was staying in the most miserable hotel. I thought, what have I done?' She met David Gross for the first time at the hotel in June 1997, and things started to look up. 'David was my inspiration and working with him was fantastic.' Which was just as well, as the factory itself was hardly encouraging. 'There were long, empty hallways, hot offices with bad lighting, and in the factory were lots of half assembled bikes. My lasting impression now is of how gritty it all was.

'Our office was like a broom closet. We had no computers, no communication devices, nobody spoke English ... it was empty and bleak, like a ghost town. On top of this there was such a weird feeling in the air. People knew I was associated with the investors and there was a lot of suspicion. No-one knew where I was coming from. So we just got down and dirty – I don't remember doing anything outside of work for the next two and half years! I worked all the time, weekends too. Leaving at 10.30pm on a Friday night was not a strange thing to do.'

Kristin and David effectively had to set up everything associated with a modern, international company from scratch, from producing brochures to establishing press relationships, and even installing proper communications systems. Ducati only started using e-mail from 2000! The pace of change was breathtaking. Within six months a clothing line had been worked out with leathers company Dainese – 'I remember driving down to Vicenza at 10 o'clock at night to look at designs!' Kristin was also organising the first World Ducati Weekend. 'Motivating Ducati was a nightmare then. I remember going around the factory with a trolley putting up WDW posters. Massimo Bordi came up to me and asked if I couldn't find someone else to do that for me. No! I couldn't!'

'I think I must have walked three or four miles a day in the first year. That factory's huge! You might need to pick up something from the receiving area, then go across to the graphics department or whatever, constantly walking. And in the middle of all this I was having to do factory tours! I'd get a call from the front desk that a group of Australians had arrived for a tour and no-one else spoke English, so I'd walk them around.' She laughs again: 'I didn't know the first thing about what I was talking about! Everyone knew a thousand times more about Ducati than I did!' But it didn't take long for the sense that she was dealing with something special to grow in Kristin. 'I'd go through the factory with people who didn't work in the industry, even other TPG portfolio people. They'd say: "God this is really weird, there's this amazing feeling in here". Yet the offices were dirty, there's nothing fancy, it's totally nuts and bolts, linoleum city!'

She recalls an incident on one of those tours: 'I recollect this guy who had an empty film canister with him. As we were walking past some of the machinery he dipped it into one of the metal waste bins to collect some swarf. It was to take home to a friend of his in Australia! These people are obsessed – I can't think of any product ever that generates that kind of dedication.

'I didn't know anything about bikes before I came to Ducati, I'd just never been exposed to them. I didn't expect any of this, so for me it was a great surprise. But it made things easier for us.'

The responsibility for what she had in her charge started to tell on Kristin when the Ducati logo had to be changed. The rights to the typeface used under the previous ownership were retained by the Cagiva Group, so there was no alternative but to change it more or less overnight. 'People wondered what was going on. They'd say we were changing the logo of their favourite product in the whole world. We got lots of nasty letters and faxes... I pinned them all up on the wall of my office! Now I think the logo looks totally natural and in tune, it's bold, aggressive, dynamic. But I remember the first bikes coming off the production line with it – there was a time when both old and new were in the delivery room and I thought oh my god, we're changing it to that!'

Kristin's influence on Ducati as a modern commercial business beyond anguishing details such as the logo change has undoubtedly been substantial. It now boasts up-to-date communications outlets with all types of media around the world, effective sales and marketing teams with defined strategies, while the moves to expand the business beyond the bikes themselves continue apace. In 2001 she was responsible for drawing in the older Ducati fans with the Motogiro event, a

modern revival of the race on open roads which Italian manufacturers once used to display the prowess of their machines, albeit at a high cost in the lives of many racers. The new Motogiro is more of a tour based around the original bikes, including those with which Ducati was especially successful from 1954 to 1957. It's in the way Kristin describes this, with eyes sparkling, that you can see how Ducati in its turn has influenced her.

'The first Motogiro was one of the most exciting events I've ever worked on for Ducati. We had a lot of famous racers – Spaggiari, Maoggi and so on, and it was really touching. These guys are die-hards, they see through everything, yet they just wanted to get on these bikes. Their enthusiasm was really moving – they didn't care about anything except being with their buddies they'd raced with and getting on old machines you didn't think would even make it to the end of one leg of the trip.

'It was a great venue for bringing in current Ducati riders to see the history – everyone who came was just blown away. It was really authentic because it was based on something that was true. You can see how special Ducati is when you hear people talking about their bikes, as if they're talking about a lover. It's not just a mode of transport – it's loaded with all the connotations of something fast, sexy and Italian, and that has included some of the problems! Ducati used to have bad trouble with the mechanics of the bikes, but because of this and being hard to get, it was a relationship which had to be cultivated. And that's why people love them.

'It's like when you have the perfect man and he does something ... you think god, I hate him! But it's also what makes you love him even more!'

Kristin works with event organisers such as the Guggenheim Museum on the Art of the Motorcycle exhibition. (Kevin Ash)

About 70,000 volatile Italians packed into the Autodromo Dino Ferrari on 23 April 1972. They were there for the inaugural Imola 200, Europe's Daytona for the Formula 750 class, a category not dissimilar to modern World Superbikes where the race bikes are based on road-going production machines, although the rules were more loose then, even allowing special one-off frames to be used. The event had caught the imagination of the manufacturers, with eleven different factories fielding or supporting entries ridden by some of the world's best riders: MV Agusta, Honda, Triumph, Norton, BSA and Moto Guzzi were all running full factory machines, while Kawasaki, BMW, Suzuki and Laverda each had factory-supported entries, with names such as Phil Read, John Cooper, Percy Tait, Walter Villa and of course, Giacomo Agostini, on board.

Oh yes, and the little Italian Ducati factory was represented too, although it wasn't that well known and the rider, Englishman Paul Smart, although he was good he wasn't spoken of in the same breath as Read and Agostini. Anyway, insiders knew that because Ducati didn't have a large budget its bikes were running road bike frames – you could even see the centre stand lugs behind the engines – and the 750cc V-twins were using standard 750GT bottom ends with quite mildly tuned top ends. Agostini meanwhile was using a four-cylinder MV Agusta with the engine breathed on by the most successful grand prix race marque to date, and the frame was taken directly from the company's 500 grand prix race bikes, as were the brakes and forks. This is a bit like slotting an HRC-tuned FireBlade engine into Mick Doohan's NSR500 chassis, and getting Mick Doohan to ride it. The racing cognoscenti knew Ducati as technically clever and successful in the smaller classes but its production bikes were only built in small numbers and it wasn't thought of as a real contender. Its first ever big capacity machine, the 750GT V-twin, had only been in production in small numbers for a year, and anyway, as that was simply based on a couple of single-cylinder top ends grafted on to the one crankcase it wasn't a serious big bike, was it?

Imagine then the atmosphere, the sheer astonishment, as on the fourth lap Smart and his Ducati swept past Agostini, in the lead on his MV, followed by second Ducati rider Bruno Spaggiari, before the two crossed the line 200 miles later, first and second!

This was the most significant race in Ducati's history, more so even than Mike Hailwood's TT

Paul Smart poised on the brink of history as he readies himself for the 200-mile race at Imola in April 1972. (Ducati)

After his improbable, fabulous victory
he witnessed the passion Ducati inspires

victory in the Isle of Man six years later, which was more about the man than about the machine. This was Ducati storming on to the world stage in the most dramatic fashion imaginable, humiliating the world's best the very first time out and proving its V-twins irrefutably in the process.

The race also convinced Ducati that it should concentrate on race classes which were related to production machines, after it had spent a few quite promising years building grand prix machines. It's a policy the company has stuck with consistently ever since with series such as World Superbikes and even now it's only moving into grands prix as the new four-stroke rules allow it to retain that road bike relevance. Yet a mere ten days before his historic victory, which would assure Smart's fame as much as Ducati's, he had no inkling that he would have any involvement whatsoever with the race or the company. He was racing in the USA at the time with the Hanson Kawasaki team, although things were not going very well. 'Money was so tight all the time, we weren't getting paid much and there wasn't enough to maintain the bikes properly. Those old air-cooled Kawasakis weren't reliable anyway, and the whole thing wasn't working out.'

Ducati meanwhile was looking for a final rider for the four-man team it was putting together for the Imola 200, and it was beginning to struggle. 'It was amazing that Ducati was even considering this race,' says Smart. 'I had the feeling that some bureaucrat in the government agency which ran Ducati, who didn't know a thing about motorcycles, came up with the idea. It's as if he thought, 'I know, we'll get lots of publicity if we win at Imola. I'll get the engineers to design a bike which will come first'! He didn't understand that you just couldn't do that...'

Smart's knee-out, and sometimes knee-down, riding position set the style used by modern racers. (Ducati)

Ducati's race director Fredmano Spairani was at least given an appropriate budget and he'd tried to sign up the best riders, including the great Finn Jarno Saarinen, Barry Sheene and Renzo Pasolini. But Ducati in 1972 was not a name associated with big capacity race bikes, despite its success in the smaller classes, and they all turned the ride down, assuming the small Bologna factory would stand no chance in its first F750 race, and they'd end up just looking rather stupid.

So Spairani was becoming desperate as the race was getting close. He had managed to sign up three riders in Ermanno Giuliano and Englishman Alan Dunscombe as well as long-time Ducati racer Bruno Spaggiari, but his brief was to put together a four-man team, and of course, to win – these riders were good, but not quite at the highest level he was after. One of the people he contacted was engine tuner Vic Camp, who immediately thought of Paul Smart, but they were unable to contact him – he was in the middle of nowhere in the USA at the time and simply couldn't be reached. So they spoke instead to Smart's wife Maggie (sister of Barry Sheene), who in light of the fact they were practically broke, did the deal on his behalf! Smart recalls his reaction: 'I was furious!' he says, expecting a Ducati V-twin to be hopelessly off the pace. 'I said, I'm not racing that bloody truck!' But he did.

An air of unreality descended as soon as he arrived at Milan airport. 'I'd been travelling from Road Atlanta circuit in Georgia for a couple of days, and I'd barely slept, my face was covered in stubble and I must have been pretty smelly by then! But I was met by a huge chauffeur-driven limo complete with black curtains at the windows like some Mafia staff car and taken straight to the test circuit at Modena. We didn't even stop off at a hotel on the way! There was only one week left to the race, I was exhausted, the bikes' frames weren't even painted, and they were fitted with Dunlop TT100 road tyres as the team didn't think race tyres would last the 200 miles of the Imola race. But I was taken aback at Ducati's set-up – after the tight Hanson Kawasaki team it was quite a shock to have some 30 staff around and ten bikes for us four riders – two each plus a couple of spares. They were naive in some ways but very serious about it.'

Smart had stopped worrying about things though. 'I wondered what the hell was going on, but by this point I had reached that strange sort of high you get when you haven't slept for ages, everything becomes sort of detached, and it didn't seem to matter.' He had never been around the circuit before and worse, the bike felt just horrible. He came back in thinking he'd been 'dog slow' but he was in for another surreal experience: 'When I rode back in to the garage they were all jumping up and down with excitement. They told me I'd been lapping faster than the record set by Agostini.' And that had been achieved on a 500cc MV Agusta grand prix bike. With race tyres!

Things got better still as the Ducati team proved to work extremely well. Changes which Smart asked for were made overnight, exactly as he'd requested and he started to get on better with the bike. His mechanic spoke as much English as Smart did Italian, which was practically none, yet they soon established an effective understanding which came of their race experience. An outsized twistgrip was fitted to accommodate Smart's injured wrist, he finally persuaded the team to fit race tyres and just days later, they were practising at Imola for the race. 'Sometimes Ago was quicker, sometimes it was us, but all the time we were on the pace.'

Spaggiari and Smart qualified in first and second places on the grid, but still he didn't feel under any great pressure. After all, he had nothing to lose in terms of reputation as the Ducatis weren't expected to get anywhere anyway. Yet they'd not just been lapping quicker than Agostini on the MV Agusta, but also the fearsomely fast two-stroke H2R Kawasakis, the legendary factory CR750 Hondas, works Triumph triples, Suzuki two-stroke triples, plus the Laverda and Moto Guzzi twins, ridden by the cream of the world's riders. There had been a promise from Spairani that he could keep the bike if he won, but it didn't hold a great deal of value for him. He and Spaggiari had also been told they would have to split the prize money equally if they came in first and second, but that seemed such a remote possibility it barely registered at the time.

The prospect of a good result receded further after the start of the race, when Smart had problems with first gear. 'I could feel the gear dogs weren't engaging properly as it kept jumping in and out of gear. This was only a lap or two into the race, so I just did without it. Imola at the time had none of the chicanes it has now – most of the curves were long, fast and sweeping, so it didn't matter much. In fact I probably went quicker using second!'

The Ducati was well suited to those Imola curves, almost suspiciously so, according to Smart.

Part of the deal with
Ducati was that Smart
could keep his race bike
(16) if he won – but not
the leathers. (Don Morley)

Donington, 2001, where Smart was deeply involved with his son Scott's race team, from management to spannering. (Kevin Ash)

'I'm convinced the bike was designed solely to win that one race,' he says. 'It was dreadfully slow turning but very, very stable, just what was needed at that circuit in those days.'

Smart and Spaggiari pulled out in front after only a handful of laps, a position they held for the best part of 200 miles, although the lead was swapping constantly between them. Right at the end of the race Spaggiari ran off the track – some observers agreed the bike was misfiring, which he claimed was because he was running out of fuel. Others thought he was trying too hard to cross the line first in front of his home crowd. Certainly he wasn't happy at coming in second. 'Bruno was upset. He'd had this great racing career with Ducati and here he was at Imola in front of 70,000 Italians on the new bike ahead of these other great names, but with me ahead of him – of course he didn't like it.' Smart was never sure what Spaggiari felt about him personally, but he has great respect for something which happened 26 years later: 'We were both on stage at the first World Ducati Weekend in 1998. Bruno took hold of the microphone and announced we were the best of buddies and gave me a big hug, as if we were sort of making up. I was really pleased.'

After that improbable, fabulous victory Smart was swept along in the most astonishing celebrations – he was even given the honorary freedom of Bologna and paraded around the city in an open-topped bus before adoring crowds. He reckons now that there must have been some 25,000 people who came out to see the Ducati riders. It was then that the enormous passion surrounding Ducati became clear to Smart. He hadn't taken much notice of things leading up to the race, he'd just concentrated on the job he'd been asked – and paid – to do. He had noticed somebody called Taglioni wandering around, not seeming to do much, but '...I only realised much later the significance of who he was. I thought then he was just hanging about, but I know now he was observing, thinking. Everything was going on inside his head.'

It was different at the factory. 'The race workshop was right at the back of the factory, the dingy end, but whenever a race bike fired up, everyone would stop work, even those on the production lines, and come out to have a look.' He has a final observation which offers an insight into the Ducati phenomenon: 'Those celebrations in the city after the race – it wasn't so much an Italian thing, more about Bologna itself. It seemed to be Bologna even above the rest of Italy.'

It is late afternoon on Sunday, 13 May 2001. The crowds at Monza are still reluctant to leave, unwilling to let go of the raw, passionate excitement which roused them to near hysteria as Australian Troy Bayliss battled aggressively with American Colin Edwards for victory in both rounds of the World Superbike race. The ending was pure fairy tale for the home fans as Ducati-mounted Bayliss twice crossed the line ahead of the American's Honda, restoring the Borgo Panigale bikes to what seemed like their birthright status at the head of the championship table.

Back in Bologna, a telephone rings. A sprightly, warm and friendly lady called Narina picks it up – the call is from a security guard. In any other situation this might have been about a lost bag, a stolen car perhaps or maybe an unattended burglar alarm. But this security guard works in the gatehouse at the Ducati factory, and Narina's husband is one Fabio Taglioni, one of the greatest motorcycle engineers of the last century, the man with whom any quest to discover the soul of Ducati, the essence of its appeal, must surely stop.

Taglioni has been unable to speak since 1998, after an operation on a throat ravaged by years of relentless smoking – there's barely a single picture of Taglioni in Ducati's extensive archive which doesn't show him with a cigarette in his hand or mouth. So Narina relays the conversation to Taglioni – it seems the guard is so overwhelmed with joy at Ducati's performance at Monza, he just couldn't help himself: he had to telephone Taglioni, to tell him he's a champion yet again. Even though it's almost two decades since 80-year-old Taglioni worked at the factory...

Narina modestly suggests to the guard that times have moved on: 'But these people racing today are so young now!'

The guard will have none of it: 'Madam, they are young, but they are still working from the foundations which your husband has achieved.'

As we discuss this, Taglioni is deeply moved, to the point of tears. The implications of that single phone call are all too clear to him. This is no senior race technician nor one of the high-level management or designers from the factory who had thought of him after that race, but, as Narina put it, '...a humble guard!', a man with no direct involvement in the production or racing of Ducati motorcycles, whose job is solely to check the credentials of visitors and look after the

Fabio Taglioni, greatest motorcycle engineer of his generation and the soul of Ducati, died aged 80 in 2001 (Roland Brown)

Even today's fiery WSB machines
have their roots in Taglioni designs

Taglioni with Narina in 1942. It was another 12 years before he joined Ducati and transformed its fortunes. (Ducati)

car park. Yet this is a man so caught up in the passion for motorcycles – for Ducati motorcycles – as to be aware not just of the men and models of today, but the architect of Ducati's history. And to care deeply about him.

So it has always been with Ducati and its people's engineer. Taglioni joined the company in 1954 when, as a 33-year-old bursting with ideas and enthusiasm, he saw this as the best opportunity to indulge his passion for producing racing motorcycles. Ducati at the time was a big, well-organised company going through a difficult period – some 600 people were being laid off because of poor sales.

The company began in 1926 when three brothers, Bruno, Adriano and Marcello had founded the Societè Scientifica Radio Brevetti Ducati to produce electrical equipment including radios which used designs and ideas patented by their father, Antonio Ducati. Ducati flourished up to the Second World War, by which time it was based in a new building designed by Bruno, on the site of the current Ducati factory in Borgo Panigale, Bologna.

The factory was destroyed by Allied bombing during the war, and afterwards the brothers, bound by restrictions on what they were allowed to produce, decided to address the urgent market for cheap transport and in 1946 produced the Cucciolo, a simple four-stroke engine which strapped to a bicycle. The design and production machinery was bought from Aldo Farinelli, a lawyer and motoring enthusiast who had set up the SIATA factory in Turin to produce the engine, but Ducati quickly began to produce its own complete bikes and, being Italian, started to race.

By the early Fifties Ducati was producing proper motorcycles, such as the single-cylinder 98, as well as the highly advanced Cruiser scooter, with hydraulic/direct drive switching, electric start and automatic gears. But by 1954 the little Cucciolo had been in production for many years and was ageing, while the Cruiser scooter was proving a disaster as it was very expensive, slow and unreliable (Taglioni dismissed it as far too complex and over-engineered). So Ducati desperately needed new designs, and it also wanted to go racing.

Taglioni was then working at Mondial with three or four other engineers in the race department, where initially he was very happy. But his ambitions fell victim to internal jealousies

which came to a head when the team 'forgot' to invite him to the victory celebrations for the 175cc race bike into whose development he'd put a huge amount of energy.

It was then that Ducati contacted Taglioni, but this wasn't his only option – Ford had been in touch with a very lucrative offer. But Taglioni's motivation was never money, Narina laughs: 'If Fabio had only ever worked according to where the best money was, we'd be millionaires by now!' They're comfortably off these days, but clearly not in that league.

Narina cites another example: 'Fabio and his team once went to Rome to test the Marianna Gran Sport, and he saw the most beautiful villa. One of the component suppliers was with him at the time, and he told Fabio, if he used the supplier's bearings, that villa would be his!

'Fabio said, "No!" What would he do with it? He had too much work to do! So they used to phone me every day to see if their bearings were working properly.' Narina laughs again: 'How would I know if their bearings were okay?'

Glamour and prestige didn't sway him either. In 1955 Taglioni was approached by Enzo Ferrari, who wanted Taglioni to work on a new desmodromic engine for his racing cars. Narina explains why he turned down the move to Maranello: 'Fabio loves engines, but with a car there are many other design aspects, such as the aerodynamics and so on. He didn't want to work on all that, and wouldn't have been able to. He didn't want to work with people who might be awkward and have other motives such as jealousy or whatever.'

Intriguingly, if he had been tempted then it would be Ferrari today, and not Ducati, which bears the standard for the desmodromic valve system. And it gives Ducati quite an advantage,

Despite his illness, Taglioni appeared at the opening of the Ducati museum in 1998, and was thrilled at his reception. (Kevin Ash)

especially as the system's close association with the Bologna bikes makes it very difficult for others to use desmodromics without facing a charge of merely copying Ducati.

So it's useful to understand exactly how desmodromic valve gear works, and why Taglioni was such an ardent proponent of the system. There have been several variations of the theme used by Taglioni, but the principle is always the same – the valves are opened by rocker arms operated from the overhead camshafts. As the lobe on the camshaft pushes the rocker arm, so that pushes open the valve. Conventional stuff, and no surprises. The difference comes in closing the valve. Instead of it being returned to the valve seat by a spring, as on every other motorcycle, a second rocker arm pulls it shut again. This closing arm has a forked end which fits around the valve stem a little below the top and which pulls against a shim shaped like a top hat, which slides over the valve stem. Once in the right place, the shim is held there by a circlip.

It's clearly important that the cam profiles are ground very accurately, as both the opening and closing rocker arms must follow exactly the same path, otherwise they could end up pulling against each other with disastrous consequences. In practice this doesn't prove to be a problem.

The advantages are considerable. In the first place, with no heavy valve springs to push against, the engine's internal friction is substantially reduced, releasing more horsepower at the back wheel as well as helping to keep mechanical noise low.

Secondly, it is possible to accelerate the valves open and closed much more violently than in a conventional engine. The valve can be held closed for longer, fired to the fully open position much more quickly, held there for longer then pulled closed much faster than usual. As a result the valve spends a larger proportion of its opening duration in the fully open position, offering less impediment to the flow of gases in or out of the engine.

The benefit is mainly to mid-range torque, though top end horsepower is also increased, and this is the real secret, if you can call it such, of Ducati's success against the Japanese four-cylinder machines in World Superbikes today. Thanks to Taglioni...

Ironically, the most frequently cited advantage of desmodromics is that they allow an engine to rev higher because the possibility of valve bounce is eliminated. This was certainly also the case in

Taglioni's earlier designs, when valve spring materials were less advanced and breakages were common, and in two-valve engines the bigger, heavier valves were more likely to float off the cams and make disastrous contact with a piston. But in modern four-valve engines piston speed determines the ceiling of engine revs, not the valve gear, so while this might have been the case twenty or thirty years ago, it's no longer so.

But those other advantages are still entirely valid, and they lead to other gains. The low friction characteristics of desmodromics are what allows the use of toothed belts for the camshaft drive, for example. These are quieter than chains or gears, require no oil and are cheaper to make, but on conventional valve spring, high performance engines they aren't reliable enough. Taglioni might have retired, but along with his spirit, even the gritty engineering details of his legacy are a powerful influence in modern Ducatis.

Back in 1954 Taglioni was taking only the first steps on this long and legendary road in front of him. His desire to work on all aspects of a project, which decided him to move to Ducati, had another angle as well as avoiding jealousies and tensions with other engineers.

Here he had full control of a team and the ability to do everything the way he wanted. He had formed his race team by selecting 10 or 15 of the best workers from the production lines, making no bones about what was expected of them – he would be intolerant of strike action or any similar difficulties and expected them to work whatever hours were needed. Racing took place over the weekends and they needed to be present – if they didn't like it, they could always return to the production lines.

This dealt with the jealousies and ego difficulties, but equally important, with this arrangement came total responsibility. Taglioni always insisted on testing the bikes himself before allowing a rider out on them – he resolutely bore as much of the risk himself as possible. These were his bikes, and just as much as it was his glory if they won, if they caused an accident so it was his fault. When Degli Antoni died at Monza on a Ducati in 1956, Taglioni was absolutely distraught.

So the idea of working at Ferrari where other engineers would be responsible for designing various aspects of the cars was never even an option as far as Taglioni was concerned. Instead,

Taglioni's philosophy was to create a complete performance package, a formula which continues to this day. (Ducati)

he immersed himself at Ducati, where the work was all-consuming. Often the mechanics would sleep on the floor of the workshop, but Taglioni would be there with them, taking the full brunt of the effort yet transmitting his unbounded enthusiasm and dedication to them in the process. Narina knows this all too well: 'We've been married for 59 years, but he would do everything on the bikes, design and test every single component himself – tutto, tutto, tutto! And when he was at Ducati I hardly saw him at all!' She says this not at all bitterly, but with great pride, a point at which once again during our interview, Taglioni is overcome with emotion. Despite the intensity of the work, there were lighter moments. Taglioni remembers racer Leopoldo Tartarini as a practical joker, recalling an incident at the Baglioni Hotel in the centre of Bologna where they were all staying. Another racer was known to have a nervous disposition, so Tartarini made himself up to look like a corpse and hid in the racer's wardrobe. When he opened the door to get his pyjamas, Tartarini fell out and slumped to the floor, causing the racer to run screaming – and naked – into the streets, only to be chased by the police!

'Still, they got their revenge,' says Narina. 'Tartarini broke his foot later on, so they threw him into the fountain at Riccione, plaster cast and all!'

Narina remembers when Mike Hailwood arrived in Italy from the Bahamas in 1958, just before Christmas. 'All he had on was a thin shirt and he was shaking with the cold,' she says. 'I took him into town and bought him a big coat, but it didn't suit him too well. When we went back, Fabio took one look at him and said, "Madonna! What big feet!" They'd never seen Mike race before,

Taglioni was known as the people's engineer for his willingness to come down to the shop floor and mix with the workers. (Ducati)

and Fabio claimed his feet were so big they'd slow him down on the bike! Afterwards we thought they must have been an asset instead... but those feet were famous!'

Yet it was during the darkest times that the Ducati workers' respect for Taglioni shone out the strongest. During a particularly unpleasant period of strikes and troubles at the factory, Ducati boss Dr Giuseppe Montano actually insisted on giving Taglioni a gun to protect himself, even though he'd said he could never shoot anyone! The workers were picketing the gates to prevent any management from entering, but this wasn't going to stop Taglioni from working. When he was confronted by hostile workers, he told them they'd have to kill him to stop him going in to the racing department.

They realised he must be Taglioni, and when he confirmed he was, their manner changed completely and they said of course he must go in. He went to work every day during this period, and without Montano knowing it took possession of the factory, persuading the workers to clean it up and even polish the floors, and when several days later the rest of the management arrived to take a look, they were astonished at the beautiful condition of the shop floor and the mild-mannered behaviour of the workers. They complimented them on this and the response was universal – this was Taglioni's doing. What he says, we do.

The loyalty from his staff was matched by admiration from his peers for his honour – Enzo Ferrari had asked Taglioni to take over development of the Dino car when his son Dino had to withdraw because of his degenerative illness. Despite the incentives, Taglioni refused, purely out of respect for the son. Yet it's not for his fine human qualities for which Taglioni is known, but his engineering genius which took Ducati to the forefront of world class motorcycle racing with a host of innovative technical solutions that has seen the relatively small Bologna factory taking on the giants of the world time and again, and coming out on top.

The battling, brilliant Taglioni legacy is more than spiritual. Even the fire-breathing World Superbike race machines of today can trace their roots back to Taglioni's last complete design, the Pantah-based 750F1.

They're still winning, and through their soul, Taglioni is still winning too.

A small, specialist motorcycle company was founded in Rimini on Italy's Adriatic coast in 1973 by three men who had made their living designing and fabricating ducting for air conditioning systems. The company name came from the first two letters of their surnames – Bianchi, Morri and Tamburini. Massimo Tamburini proved not just his talent at Bimota with such superb designs as the Kawasaki-powered KB2 and the Ducati-engined DB1 (a bike which turned the flagging company's fortunes around in the mid-1980s), but also his basic philosophy which he adheres to as much today as ever: 'I met an engineer from Suzuki in Japan once who asked me what I thought bikes should be like in the future. I said the ideal one would be a 750 with the power of a 1000 and the weight of a 500. You don't need a huge amount of power for a road bike, but it's important to have light weight as well.'

It's a conviction which dovetailed perfectly into Ducati's way of thinking. Tamburini had stayed with Bimota for 11 years, and after a brief spell with the Gallina 500 grand prix team was taken on in 1985 by the ambitious Cagiva Group, owned by the Castiglioni brothers. This was the same year that Cagiva took control of Ducati after its years of decay under Italian state ownership, and Tamburini set to work on designing Ducatis as well as Cagivas.

His first Ducati was the Paso 750, an innovative design with fully enclosing bodywork but one which suffered from poor carburation, although this was cured with the later 907ie. But it was in 1993 that Tamburini's most famous creation was unveiled, one of the most influential machines of the last twenty years, the Ducati 916. This epochal machine looked so good and performed so well, the aura surrounding it reached a self-generating, almost mythical status, to the point where it's practically vying with ancient legends for a place in the catalogue of the miracles of history.

In fact, surprisingly, the 916's styling was rather derivative. But it wasn't influenced by Pierre Terblanche's beautiful Supermono which was shown the previous year, as many people believe. Terblanche himself explains: 'I was working on the Supermono at the same time as Tamburini was doing the 916. We were both in the Cagiva Research Centre (CRC) in San Marino and it was he who influenced me, not the other way around. It just so happened that the Supermono was shown to the public first.'

Massimo Tamburini broke all the existing rules about how bikes should be created. (Gold & Goose)

Tamburini has this deep understanding
of engineering as well as design

With the 916 Tamburini and his team combined poise, aggression and championship-winning power. *(Two Wheels)*

But there was a bike before the 916 which featured the same high rise, underseat exhaust layout with a single-sided swingarm, designed to visually isolate the fat rear wheel, plus a pair of letterbox headlights and a profile, when viewed from above, exhibited an unmistakably female hourglass figure. The bike was even painted red...

Such a shame that the exotic Honda NR750 – this was the machine in question – was so fabulously expensive yet performed so ordinarily, otherwise many more people might have seen beyond its oval pistons, its eight valves per cylinder and its paired conrods and recognised an entirely new look which was both thoroughly original and extraordinarily attractive. And, as the 916 illustrates, extremely influential.

Tamburini at the time (the NR750 was unveiled in Autumn 1991) had been working on the design of Ducati's new sports bike which was to replace the 888 for nearly two years, and was already well on the way to finalising the shape of the 916 when he saw the NR750 for the first time, and it was definitely not looking like the bike we know so well today. All the man himself will admit is that he was influenced by existing designs, which is no admission at all, as all designers inevitably are influenced by what's around them. So speak to others who were working with Tamburini, such as current Ducati design chief Pierre Terblanche (who has enormous admiration for Tamburini) and while they won't say as much, neither will they deny it, and it becomes clear that when the NR750 appeared it was responsible for some rapid rethinking in the CRC.

Let's keep this in perspective though. The NR750 might be the originator of the distinctive look now so commonly associated with the 916, but still Tamburini moved it forward, personalised and Ducati-fied it, in particular with his blend of sharp edges and sweeping curves which, like most innovation, broke existing rules about how things should be done. In particular, Tamburini understands as the Honda's designers did not, how important is the visual weight of a bike, of where to make it appear bulky or substantial, and where to keep the shapes looking slender or unobtrusive. Combine this with the narrow frontal area that Ducati's engineers prefer for its low aerodynamic drag, and the company's strong, distinctive yet delicate-looking steel trellis frame, and the result is a shape which is both muscular, aggressive and intimidating and yet feline almost to the point of femininity. The magic Tamburini touch was to endow the 916 with all of this from whichever angle it is viewed, a task known as notoriously difficult among motorcycle designers.

So far we've covered only the look of the 916, and if it seems to have influences from elsewhere, the fundamental engineering of the bike owes nothing to any manufacturer other than Ducati itself, and in this respect it is an entirely predictable evolution of Ducati's technology. Which, it shouldn't be forgotten, has dominated World Superbike racing since the bike first competed in 1994. The 916 was the product of a genius working for a unique company, and for those who thought the staggering good looks of the bike might be an accidental one-off, Tamburini proved them wrong by producing a second amazingly beautiful machine in the MV Agusta F4, after the Castiglioni brothers split from Ducati and revived this other famous Italian marque. But without the Ducati engineering the MV has never been, nor has it tried to be, the phenomenal track success of the 916.

Yet Tamburini is self taught. 'I have always had this huge passion for motorcycles – my mother used to complain about it when I was a little boy, calling it my obsession! I have never had any desire to design anything else.' But Tamburini has very strong ideas about what constitutes a real Ducati. 'It must not mimic the Japanese, and it must blend form and function – these two are inseparable.' Which is why he is not in favour of some other Ducati models: 'I think the ST2 is an attempt to follow a Japanese concept, and this shouldn't be done by Italians.'

But whether or not he agrees with everything the modern Ducati is doing, those at Ducati are well aware of Tamburini's great strengths as a designer. Terblanche knows as well as anyone: 'Tamburini has this deep understanding of engineering as well as design, which is why he is able to combine the two so effectively.' Tamburini is no longer with Ducati, having decided to stay with the Castiglionis when they were forced to sell the company in 1996 and continues with the Cagiva Group, which became MV Agusta in 1999.

He will continue to be missed, his huge contributions adding another glorious chapter to the compulsive Ducati story. But his departure shows something else – since the days of Taglioni the Ducati story has no longer been that of one man.

Tamburini's passion for design goes back to a boyhood obsession for which his mum scolded him! (Gold & Goose)

As far as Carl Fogarty's inner circle of associates are concerned – and his wife Michaela – Davide Tardozzi is the best race team manager the Englishman has ever had. Fogarty himself agrees, and to observers of the sport, commentators and fans, Tardozzi is well known as the man who reinstilled the fight into Fogarty when he seemed to be faltering in 1998, firing him up enough to go on to win the world title in this and the following year.

It's an oddly rare thing in any sport for a top-line competitor to switch to team management and make a great success of it, but that's exactly what Tardozzi did. Although he never won a World Superbike championship, he came close. Indeed, Tardozzi has the honour of being the first rider ever to take the chequered flag in a World Superbike race, crossing the line ahead of the field on his works Bimota YB4 in the inaugural race at Donington in 1988, although as the round was decided on an aggregate basis and Tardozzi crashed out in the second leg, he didn't actually win.

Bimota's race effort in 1989 was muddled and ineffective, but Tardozzi meanwhile had become involved with Franco Farnè in the development of the Ducati 888 superbike racer – although Tardozzi was known as a regular crasher in the heat of racing, Farnè always trusted his judgement in setting up a bike.

It was this crashing habit of Tardozzi's which prevented him taking the championship in 1988, as he'd won the most number of races. But partly because of Farnè's recommendation Ducati took him on in 1990 in one of its satellite teams, and in 1992, he became the test rider for the works race bikes, a pretty demanding job as the factory was running six official bikes at that point!

As well as this, Tardozzi was deeply involved with Massimo Tamburini in the development of Ducati's forthcoming but still secret weapon, the 916, subsequently the most successful World Superbike race machine ever, for which he is undoubtedly partly responsible. He can also boast another first: 'I was the first person ever to ride the 916 road bike on a race track when I took it out at Mugello. I couldn't believe it! I thought wow, that's a race bike!'

Okay, Tardozzi didn't quite think 'Wow!' – his English generally is good but he's a master of some of the earthier expressions in our language, which are probably best not printed here... But however he expresses it, it's clear he loved the bike. 'It felt very different at first, and the looks

Davide Tardozzi has a great talent for getting his riders focused on the challenge ahead. (Gold & Goose)

This team manager is famous for
putting the **fight** back into Fogarty

were amazing. But because I was involved in the development, the bike was basically shaped around me.' So all you 916 riders out there complaining of wrist ache, back ache or whatever, it's all the fault of this small Italian – sit him on a 916 and it fits perfectly!

But it was also on one of these bikes in June 1993 when he suffered yet another crash, and just like that, he decided to quit riding. When he said quit, he meant it: 'I have never ridden a motorcycle since. I've missed riding sometimes for sure, but I haven't done it again.'

Just one thing might tempt him to swing a leg over a motorcycle seat once more though,

as Ducati begins its preparations to build and then race a grand prix bike according to the new regulations designed to allow four-strokes to compete with the dominant two-strokes: 'I have one dream now, which is to be the first person to ride the new Ducati grand prix bike!'

After his final crash (unless he manages to drop a Ducati grand prix bike in the future) Tardozzi went straight into team management, scoring the privilege of running the Grottini team, the only one outside the factory to get the works 926cc engines. Ducati clearly valued his management skills as he was entrusted with top Spanish rider Juan Garriga, as well as the highly respected racer, Stephane Mertens. But neither of these excellent riders was Tardozzi's first choice – at the beginning of the season he had been on the phone to Carl Fogarty, but factory team manager Raymond Roche scooped up the British rider just ahead of him for his own squad.

Tardozzi continued to impress with his now obvious talent for team management at the Austrian Promotor Ducati team in 1995 and 1996, where he helped Troy Corser to the World Championship in 1996 ahead of arch rival Virginio Ferrari's factory Ducati team. In 1998 Ducati

Tardozzi, no mean racer himself, could have won a World Superbike title if he'd calmed his crash or win style. (Gold & Goose)

had a difficult political problem – it found itself with popular Italian rider Pier-Francesco Chili, World Champion Troy Corser and former World Champion Carl Fogarty. The solution was to form a second team called Ducati Performance backed by tuning company Gia.Co.Moto, which ran only Fogarty in the Superbikes (and Paolo Casoli on the 748 in the supporting Supersport class). Fogarty came out on top with the championship – after Tardozzi's famous remotivation, but he doesn't see there was any particular magic to it though: 'Carl had quit inside himself. He was not finding the motivation which had once been his drive. He had always ridden just for himself, to prove to himself he was the best. By 1998 he had decided it was done, he had proved that.'

How then did Tardozzi change Fogarty's attitude? 'I kicked him up the arse! Okay, not all the time. I just happened to say the right things at the right time and make him believe in himself once more. I spent time with him, talking about the future. I think that's what did it.'

Tardozzi's arse kicking disguises the extremely delicate task he was carrying out – a kick at the wrong time would have alienated Fogarty forever, but Tardozzi managed to balance this with gentler talking at the same time as dealing with the huge demands of a World Championship-winning race team. He works mainly with the riders themselves rather than dealing with the technical details which others in his team concentrate on – a team which typically will have 36 people working for it at a foreign Superbike round, and for which Tardozzi is responsible. The arrival of the Ducati team in a race paddock is an impressive sight, first as the giant red race transporters are backed into position, then as their contents are spewed out in wheeled cabinets, transforming the bleak, empty shells of the pit garages into seething, busy workshops. Technicians swarm through the garages setting up state-of-the-art tools, equipment, computer monitors, data logging electronics and everything else it takes to feed the awesome demands of a world championship winning race team. There's a casual professionalism to the process borne of much practice which can look haphazard and disorganised, but at the end of a long day the pit is ready and the machinery of Tardozzi's organisation spins smoothly into life.

Yet his involvement in the detail here and in the preparation of the bikes themselves is indirect, so although he is often the one who enforces or argues decisions on tyre choices, for example, it is others who are collating the technical reasoning behind those choices. His greater concerns are for the welfare of the riders: 'If I see a rider is being troubled too much by a photographer I will step in and clear them away.' It looks to the outsider almost like some sort of paternal drive rather than simply the role of a team manager, and Tardozzi sees more to it as well: 'Ducati is different to the other companies. Everyone working here for Ducati Corsa (the race team) is not just an employee but a fan of Ducati motorcycles as well. It's a different approach to the others, and you can see and feel this difference.

'People wonder why it is like this. Why is anyone a fan of Manchester United? It's because you have followed the team, you like the players, and we do understand this is the same with football clubs. I am a fan of the Milan club and the captain of the team came to see us during a race, and we found there was a lot that was the same. And this is the difference with Ducati compared to the other factories. Honda has fans too, but they are fans of the riders, not the bikes. With us we have Ducati fans more than fans of the riders. It is the Ducati people which make it like this. We have had the same people for many years, which helps. In other teams no-one knows the people, or they change very often. But at Ducati we are like a family, and Taglioni is our grandfather!'

Like many others at Ducati, Tardozzi has only praise for the Castiglioni brothers, owners of Ducati before the American takeover in 1996, seeing them still very much as members of this family even though they are no longer directly involved. 'The brothers did something which was very good in saving Ducati and keeping us in racing, and we have to thank them for that.

'But the difference with the Americans is that TPG really organised things. The problem before was always organisation and it was getting more and more difficult, so they came along at just the right moment. Now we are planning for three, four, five years ahead! And you can be sure those things we are planning really will happen.'

So what about Tardozzi himself, who is he doing this for – Tardozzi or his Ducati family? 'I don't care about anything but winning,' as his straw bale/chequered flag race career underlines. 'I do this for me, but it's Ducati which provides the opportunity for this to happen, so I am winning for Ducati too.'

The passion of the Ducati
pit garage is captured in
the tense faces of Davide
Tardozzi and Michaela
Fogarty. (Gold & Goose)

'I wasn't born here, Italian isn't my main language, my family isn't here, I've come thousands of miles to work here!' Pierre Terblanche clearly isn't at Ducati just because there happened to be a job going. But the route to his current position as Ducati's head of design has been circuitous and included some fortuitous turns on the way.

He was born and brought up in the shadow of Cape Town's spectacular Table Mountain, and it was there while still at school that he knew he wanted some sort of involvement in vehicle design: 'The bug really bit back in 1971 when I saw the new Ferrari Modena for the first time, styled by Pininfarina. When I saw that car I knew design was what I really wanted to do.' School was followed by an unrelated three-year graphic design course – it wasn't what he wanted to do exactly, but this was the nearest he could get while still having some likelihood of getting a job afterwards. In South Africa at the time there simply weren't the opportunities in vehicle design.

Ambitions in any direction had to be put on the back burner anyway after the graphic design course, as it was straight into two years of compulsory military service, a requirement of most South African men, followed by a five-year stint with the huge Young & Rubicam advertising agency's Cape Town office. But in an unlikely twist of fate, quite by chance while there Terblanche met Giorgietto Giugiaro of the famous Italian car design company – both were attending a conference on plastics. After confessing his real desire to get into car design, Terblanche was encouraged enough by Giugiaro to give up his job and attend the vehicle design course at the Royal College of Art in South Kensington, London (source of many of the world's best-known car and motorcycle designers). He managed to procure sponsorship from Ford Germany, his mentor being Patrick Le Quement who has since gone on to become the highly successful chief of design at Renault.

So why did Terblanche go from the RCA to work at VW, not Ford? He smiles almost sheepishly: 'I don't think I did enough nice sketches for Ford! They were really into that and I wasn't.'

Three and a half years with VW working mainly on the design of car interiors was further valuable real world training, but Terblanche always had one eye open for any opportunities in the motorcycle world. He had, after all, a deep passion for motorcycles, long before there was any

Pierre Terblanche has to maintain the traditions of gorgeous style and fabulous performance. (Roland Brown)

The design chief who looks
to the future as well as the past

possibility of working for a bike factory. Even in his early twenties there was always a special place for Ducati, the seeds of which were sown in 1977 when Cook Neilson won at Daytona. This was another highly significant race in Ducati's history, one which got the company noticed in a big way in America – as related earlier, Neilson was editor of *Cycle* magazine at the time and his modified 750SS was privately prepared without any support from the importer or factory, yet against some of the best official BMWs, Kawasakis and so on, he won the Superbike race at an average speed of just over 100mph, clocking a top speed a fraction under 150mph in the process. 'That was just fantastic,' says Terblanche. 'I thought, that's the bike for me! The year after that Hailwood scored his fantastic victory on the Isle of Man, and I collected all the articles I could on him. I owned a Ducati 750GT at the time, but I'd always wanted to redesign it. My idea for it was very weird, like a big insect. But I never took it beyond just the sketches. To do that for real would have been absolute perfection, but I never dreamed I would be in a position to do so!'

In the end, the first move from VW didn't involve a great deal of effort – Terblanche had always admired Massimo Tamburini's Ducati 750 Paso ever since he saw it at the 1985 Milan Show, so he simply picked up the telephone and called him. By this time Tamburini was working for Cagiva-Ducati, and Terblanche's next step was to turn up there himself – he was given a job! 'That's how it works in Italy!' he says. He started off with Tamburini in Rimini, then moved to Cagiva's factory in Varese where he designed his first Ducati, the innovatively engineered Supermono racing single.

Although the Supermono was unveiled before Tamburini's 916, prompting some to speculate

Terblanche's inspirations came from Neilson's 1977 victory at Daytona and the work of Massimo Tamburini. (Kevin Ash)

that Terblanche inspired the great Italian designer, he says not. 'We were working on both bikes at the same time, and I was influenced by him, not the other way around.'

In the early 1990s Cagiva set up its specialist design studio, the Cagiva Research Centre (CRC) in San Marino near Tamburini's home in Rimini. Terblanche moved there, where he designed the Cagiva Canyon and Gran Canyon before finally going to Ducati in Bologna in December 1996, a few months after Cagiva sold Ducati to the Texas Pacific Group. Tamburini had decided to remain with Cagiva, where he went on to design the acclaimed MV Agusta F4, leaving the position of design chief open. Terblanche couldn't resist – this man with his twin passions for designing motorcycles and for the Ducati marque was faced with the possibility of being in charge of designing Ducati motorcycles!

His first ever Ducati road bike however had to be produced within some tight financial and design restrictions – for 1998 Terblanche produced a completely revamped 900SS, the culmination of years of development which led directly back to Taglioni's Pantah. Up to 1998 the 900SS was looking very dated, rather underpowered and had poor low rev manners. The engineers replaced the carburettors with fuel injection and made other transmission changes, which addressed that problem, while Terblanche's role was really restricted to restyling the bodywork.

He succeeded in modernising the look of the bike, but sales weren't as strong as Ducati had hoped, largely due to a perception that the bike's basic technology was too old – its 80bhp output was low for a 1990s 900cc machine. But the bike does give some clues about how Terblanche sees Ducati design: 'The new SS was very much an evolution of the original, not really a replacement. We raised the profile at the back by lightening the rear of the frame, to give it a more aggressive look, but basically we eschewed fashion and built on Ducati's tradition. This is especially important with the SS as that's it's main strength whereas the superbikes can afford to be more cutting edge.

'I didn't want all the hard edges which are so much a part of contemporary design – for me, the SS was all about voluptuous forms, organic shapes and curves. Look at the way the shapes merge from one end of the bike to the other – it's one, continuous shape.'

He's also pleased with what the Americans have been able to achieve with the 900SS, seeing this as the first bike to really display the improvements in quality. 'I think the 900SS in 1998 was the best made Ducati up to that date.' As a designer in Italy, Terblanche reckons he's allowed more independence than he would have in many other countries, but there are important constraints and boundaries, as he points out: 'At Ducati we have more freedom than the Japanese, but this doesn't mean we can start with a fresh sheet with each bike because of the history and the need for continuity. This is very important because it's what makes Ducati what it is. We must always keep some links with the past while moving to the future.

'We each do much more of a bike than the Japanese, and with that comes more responsibility for a whole range of things other designers don't have to worry about. While designing the bike which will follow the 916 I'm also installing a whole new computer design system.'

It's here that we're reminded of the awesome responsibility of the job a Ducati design chief has, with such seminal machines as the 916 setting the company's standards, a bike which has been named motorcycle of the century in many polls, which has dominated World Superbike racing, which has appeared in museums, design exhibitions and fashion magazines where it's regularly acclaimed for its beauty, poise, performance. Isn't the job of Ducati design chief rather daunting?

'Well, yes! We have to match up to these things and also to move forward in every respect, especially in ergonomics and aerodynamics.' Ergonomics is an area where Terblanche has strong ideas – he's six feet four tall and so fully understands the difficulty of making a motorcycle fit himself as well as riders at the other end of the scale. He feels that motorcycles must start to approach the levels of adjustability which are the norm in cars, but he doesn't expect each new bike from Ducati to be a radical leap forward: 'You simply can't do that with every new model you produce. New bikes should have new features and ideas and be more advanced technically, but they must be clearly evolutions of existing designs. This links the future to the past, and it's a great strength of Ducati.'

Terblanche also sees attention to detailing as an area where Ducati can distinguish its machines, and says it's an important difference between much Italian design and what you find elsewhere. 'There's something which translates from Italian into English as the "Boy Effect". You

Terblanche maintains a sense of continuity, evolving existing models rather than replacing them. (Kevin Ash)

might see a woman of the night who really catches your eye, but when you get close and see the detail she becomes much less attractive.' He laughs at the analogy: 'It's the same with many bikes, where some components don't seem to be styled at all, and end up spoiling the overall machine.

'I wouldn't single out any particular bikes or manufacturers, but take a look at rear mudguards... Clearly with some there's no styling been involved at all, they're just big ugly, functional lumps of plastic! An engineer has been told that a mudguard is needed and he's produced one which works but without ever consulting a stylist.'

Even so, the attention to detail on Terblanche's pet project, the MH900e, borders on the obsessive. For example, the cross-section of the spokes on the MHe's wheels is the same as that on the Campagnolos fitted to Mike Hailwood's TT-winning 900SS of 1978, the bike which was the inspiration to create it. Then there are the machined aluminium housings for the brake fluid reservoirs, the delightful alloy pylons locating the screen on to the fairing, the sweeping NCR race team silver and red paint (Hailwood's bike was in red and green Castrol colours, so Terblanche went for the official Ducati livery instead), the chunky cast aluminium headlight surround, more cast aluminium for the plate atop the fuel tank, the quite gorgeous dash layout with central chrome bezel tachometer and no apparent speedometer until you switch on the ignition, when a digital one appears beneath it.

The matt cast aluminium engine sump, mimicking that of the old SS machines, is a dummy, housing electrics instead of oil, while the tubular steel, single-sided swingarm is a fabulous extension of the frame's red lattice work, designed to outline the engine's rear cylinder in the left side rear three-quarter view.

'This bike went from initial sketch to show bike in a matter of weeks, which is incredibly fast, but I've had the idea in my head for 14 years.' That idea was to create a bike which blended a host of styling cues from that most famous TT machine, with forward-looking design which would lift the bike out of the mere retro mould into a niche of its own.

If ever a man's inner feelings could be sculpted into a three dimensional object, then the MH900e is what Terblanche's passion looks like.

The MH900e took styling cues from Hailwood's 900SS, and epitomises the Terblanche attention to detail. (Kevin Ash)

The most famous, improbable, fairy tale race win there has ever been in motorcycling history, ahead even of Paul Smart's victory at Imola in 1972, came in 1978 at the Isle of Man TT. The greatest racer of them all, Mike Hailwood, was making a comeback to the island that had played such a major role in forging the legendary career in which he had won 76 grands prix and nine World Championship titles. He'd won three British championships at the age of just 18 followed by four the next year, the first man to win three Isle of Man TT races in the one week, and all on an astonishingly wide variety of machinery, from MV Agustas, Hondas, Triumphs, BSAs, to Suzukis, Mondials, Morinis and many others, including, of course, Ducatis.

Why then was his victory in the 1978 TT F1 race on the Isle of Man improbable? Because by this time Hailwood was now 38 years old, he hadn't ridden a motorcycle competitively for seven years nor raced at the Island for 11 years, and in the interim he had worked his way into car racing until, in a crash at the Nürburgring in 1974 while driving for McLaren, he badly damaged his leg, an injury he was still carrying in 1978. It was also in Formula One that Hailwood added a George Medal, the highest civilian award for bravery, to the British Empire Medal he'd won in 1968 for services to motorcycle sport. This was in recognition of how he saved the life of Clay Regazzoni in the South African Grand Prix by pulling him unconscious from his burning car, despite Hailwood catching fire himself as the fuel tanks blazed.

So here was this hero in 1978, hugely admired and to top it all, universally acclaimed as a thoroughly friendly, likeable, unassuming character, but surely by now well past his best and standing little chance of major success, down to ride not a factory machine but the private entry of motorcycle dealership Sports Motorcycles, owned and run by Steve Wynne.

According to Wynne, there was a lot more than Hailwood's reputation resting on this race: 'The previous year at the Island we had been campaigning a 900SS Ducati endurance racer which the factory had sold to us on the strength of our good performance in 1976. Roger Nicholls was leading the race, a six-lap one in which we would only need to stop to refuel once. Honda, with Phil Read riding, needed two pit stops, and it was clear we were going to win because in the first stop they found their bike had used loads of oil – it wasn't going to last the full race. So they apparently

Wynne and Hailwood met by chance, yet the partnership scored a win that made motorcycle history. (Steve Wynne)

The fairytale victory that was sweet revenge
for Wynne and Hailwood

managed to persuade the organisers to get the race shortened due to bad weather – in fact it was improving – which the organisers did without telling anyone else! Even Read knew nothing about it. The race was stopped on lap four, only one lap after our long pit stop and before Honda were due to make their second one, and we had no idea this was going to happen. We only lost by three seconds, but I was not happy!'

Hailwood himself had his own reasons for wanting to get one over on Honda. He'd been considering a TT comeback but Honda had turned him down, effectively saying he was past it, so his own motive was strong, too. But he ended up on the Sports Motorcycles Ducati almost by accident: 'After the 1977 TT we were at Silverstone when Hailwood came up to us in the pits – he was just chatting to a mutual friend, I didn't really know him then. He was just looking over the Ducati and said that this was the old type bike he was more used to, and laughingly said he wouldn't mind doing a TT on it. I said, "go on then!" and that was that. It was typical of Mike that we just shook hands on the deal – the fee was dealt with afterwards and it wasn't very much really. He had offers later when people realised he wanted to race at the Island again but even though they were for a lot more money I knew he wouldn't go back on our agreement.'

The plan originally was for Hailwood to be entered anonymously – they were going to use the name Edgar Jessop as a personal joke – because he only wanted to do it for the fun of it. But word got out and the interest became fantastic. 'I remember *Motor Cycle News* ran a photo of the engine which they'd printed in reverse. I got 20 letters or more from people saying we'd lock-wired the sump plug the wrong way around, and some people threatened to hold me responsible

They planned to race anonymously, but there was no chance. Word got out and media interest exploded. (Steve Wynne)

if Hailwood was hurt on our bike!' Ducati was taking Sports Motorcycles more seriously now anyway as they'd showed such promise on their previous Island outings and agreed to supply them with two new bikes rather than an old endurance racer, and also to get them to England in good time. This allowed Steve plenty of time to prepare the engines – the second was for Nicholls, who Wynne admits even he thought had a better chance of winning than Hailwood.

Wynne had plenty of time to work on the engines and made many alterations, including the fitment of bigger valves, different pistons, a Lucas Rita ignition system, a revised clutch and importantly, a new gearbox. 'Hewland Gears, who did a lot of Formula One car gears, made the gear cluster for us, and they didn't even charge because it was for Mike Hailwood! It would have been enormously expensive otherwise.' The engine worked well during practice, as Hailwood broke the lap record at 111mph with no problems – he thought he was only doing around 105mph laps, so easy was the bike to ride – but two factory technicians had come out to the Island as much to observe as to help, and they became very worried at how many miles the engine was accumulating before the real race. 'Franco Farnè and Giuliano Pedretti were there and they suggested we use the new factory engine they'd brought with them. It wasn't as quick as our engine, but it did the job.'

It did the job all right, but only just. In a moment which would be written off as too corny for a film script, the engine failed the moment Hailwood backed off the throttle as he crossed the finish line! Wynne wasn't even aware of this: 'After the race the bikes were taken away to be checked over by officials for legality. I was very worried that ours would fail the noise tests as these were very strict that year, and when an official said to me, "The bike won't start, will it?" I thought that was his way of helping us to avoid a noise test so he wouldn't be the one to disqualify Hailwood! I agreed of course, not realising he really meant it!'

Once again, a Ducati had won against the odds, this time beating the great Phil Read on his works Honda, a bike with at least 20hp more than the Italian machine. And what sweet revenge it was personally for Wynne and Hailwood, pushing the Japanese factory into second place with their privately funded effort and avenging the unpleasant defeat the previous year as well as Honda's slighting of Hailwood. Typically of Ducati under its state ownership, just as with Smart's victory in

1972, it was painfully slow to cash in on the unprecedented publicity Hailwood's win had generated. It was more than a year before a Hailwood Replica road bike was introduced, and with the factory's funds being desperately short this amounted to no more than a now ageing 900SS with a new fairing and fuel tank. The red and green colour scheme of the bike incidentally, was nothing to do with the Italian flag, as many people believe. 'Mike was being sponsored by Castrol and all I did was take the scheme off a Castrol oil can!' says Wynne. Even so, the importance of the Hailwood Replica shouldn't be underestimated – Ducati went on to sell around 7,000 examples over the following seven years, which quite probably saved the company from extinction. Instead, it kept going long enough for the Castiglioni brothers to step in and turn its fortunes around.

Ducati has another reason to feel indebted to Steve Wynne. His involvement with the marque had started in the early 1970s when Sports Motorcycles was looking for a franchise to take over from the failing British ones. Wynne plumped for Ducati: 'The bikes were a good, characterful alternative to the Japanese at the time, and I even raced a 750SS myself, two years after Smart's victory at Imola. I'd always wanted to win at the Isle of Man too, but had no illusions – I was a good national rider but I'd only win the TT as a dealer or sponsor!'

That he did of course with that truly historic TT win, but less well known is his role in the career of another rather well-known Ducati rider. Carl Fogarty's first ever World Superbike win was on a Steve Wynne motorcycle. 'Carl and his father bought the first bike in 1992 from us but it was wrecked at Albecete in Spain. To be fair the bikes were very fragile then and this wasn't a surprise. So Sports Motorcycles sponsored him by providing the replacement, and I did all the work on the bike, travelling with the team, and it was on our bike that he won that second leg at Donington.'

Wynne's involvement with Ducati has lasted for three decades, but it's not just because these happened to be the most convenient or even the best bikes he could get: 'I've been completely indoctrinated by Ducati! But it's not always been easy – I think it's more like falling in love and then getting married. There are lots of ups but plenty of downs, too. It's the best way though, far more interesting than everything droning along in a completely predictable way all the time. I've always felt with Ducati I've been able to have a real and personal influence, partly in selling and marketing

the bikes, but in other ways too. They still use Omega pistons for example, which I introduced them to, and there were gearbox design changes I suggested which they took on board.'

Wynne is pleased with the changes going on at Ducati today, saying the improvements in quality are considerable. 'In the last four years the quality has got better and better, and I like the way the Americans seem to be running the company. They need to let the Italians get on with the design and ideas while they do the running of the company, and that's just the way it's happening.' Yet there are some who in similar circumstances might now be bitter. He was promised royalties on the Hailwood Replica road bikes which never materialised, but that sort of thing doesn't bother Wynne. 'The royalties never came through, although the factory was in a bad state financially at the time. Maybe they would have if I had reminded them, but then Mike was killed in a road accident and it seemed inappropriate to press the matter. I didn't want to feel I'd be profiting from someone who had died.'

Wynne anyway sees this sort of thing as part of the vagaries that seem to come from dealing with Italians more interested in passion and the bigger picture than the details of business deals. 'It was always my choice to go racing and to use Ducatis, I never had to do it. And all right, so if people say Ducati has benefited so much from my efforts, so have I benefited enormously from Ducati. It's their bikes I've been using which came from their research and development which I could never possibly hope to do myself.' But much as Ducati has featured in Wynne's life, so his place is assured in the history of the company: Hailwood's 1978 TT win and a part in Fogarty's Ducati career... No wonder he's always welcome at the Bologna factory.

Steve Wynne on the 1979 Hailwood Ducati racing at Daytona in 1982. His link with Ducati lasted thirty years. (Steve Wynne)

© Kevin Ash 2001

All rights reserved. No part of this publication
may be reproduced, stored in a retrieval system
or transmitted, in any form or by any means,
electronic, mechanical, photocopying, recording
or otherwise, without prior permission in writing
from the publisher.

First published in November 2001

A catalogue record for this book
is available from the British Library

ISBN 1 85960 686 5

Library of Congress
catalog card no. 2001 132578

Published by Haynes Publishing, Sparkford,
Nr Yeovil, Somerset BA22 7JJ, England

Tel: 01963 442030  Fax 01963 440001
Int. tel: +44 1963 442030
Int. fax  +44 1963 440001
E-mail: sales@haynes-manuals.co.uk
Web site: www.haynes.co.uk

Haynes North America, Inc.,
861 Lawrence Drive, Newbury Park,
California 91320, USA

*Leather on jacket and contents page
specially made by The Leatherworkshop*

*Cover/page 3 Fogarty picture: Gold & Goose
This page: Gold & Goose*

Designed by Simon Larkin
Printed and bound in England
by J. H. Haynes & Co. Ltd, Sparkford